Free Will

Central Problems of Philosophy

Series Editor: John Shand

This series of books presents concise, clear, and rigorous analyses of the core problems that preoccupy philosophers across all approaches to the discipline. Each book encapsulates the essential arguments and debates, providing an authoritative guide to the subject while also introducing original perspectives. This series of books by an international team of authors aims to cover those fundamental topics that, taken together, constitute the full breadth of philosophy.

Forthcoming titles include

Free Will

Graham McFee

First published in 2000 by Acumen

Acumen Publishing Limited
17 Fairfax Road
Teddington
TW11 9DJ
www.acumenpublishing.co.uk

ISBN: 1-902683-04-8 (hardcover)
ISBN: 1-902683-05-6 (paperback)

British Library Cataloguing-in-Publication Data
A catalogue record for this book is available from
the British Library.

Designed and typeset by Kate Williams, Abergavenny.
Printed and bound by Biddles Ltd., Guildford and King's Lynn.

Contents

Preface and acknowledgements

While an undergraduate, I became aware of both the interest and the intractability of the problem of free will: a small prize was offered in the philosophy department for any undergraduate who presented a solution to that problem that would satisfy any two members of the department; at least, we undergraduates believed in such a prize. (Two members were required, obviously, to stop the candidates simply replaying his or her own preferred solution back to a particular staff member, as though that might have been convincing even for one!) This prize was not won during my tenure as undergraduate and research student.

Part of the attractiveness of the topic, though, was its ability to grab the attention of beginners – to show them what philosophical issues were and why they were quite generally important. Therefore this was a suitable topic for use (as here) to introduce relative beginners to philosophical issues and methods. Moreover, one's point of final arrival could be a long way into philosophy. Thus here, although issues broached and methods offered derive from Anglo-American analytical philosophy, the conclusions reached, and the conception of the philosophical enterprise subtended, are not: at least, not ones dominant in the current incarnation of that tradition (see Chapter 9)

Such a way of writing, displaying (and commenting on) both arguments and argumentative strategies, could seem like giving students "target practice" on philosophical views. This misleading picture of how philosophy should operate leaves out the crucial ways in which constructing and commenting on arguments (and drawing distinctions) can elaborate one's understandings of any position, permitting consideration of internal consistencies for such positions: if I accept/assert that, can I also accept this? And here the response may involve noting differences between the *this* and the *that*. Although clearer when seen directly in the laying-out of opponents' views, this point applies throughout the text, not just where it is highlighted explicitly. This text also illustrates that the primary concern of philosophy is not with words only, but with human perplexities.

The central difficulty here concerns the possibility of genuine agency: hence the expressions "freedom of the will" and "freedom of action" are treated as equivalent. In particular, I address the possibility of action or agency, rather than the scope and limits of such agency, although there are a number of interesting puzzles or issues there too. My explanation of this direction, expanded in the body of the book, is that discussion of the limits of agency presupposes the possibility of agency: and there seems reason not to presuppose this, reason provided by our determinist argument. If, in the end, we conclude that human agency is possible, this is once we have faced (and learned from) determinism.

Other concerns might be (and have been) given the title "problem of free will": again, the justification of my problem (the problem addressed in this work) should suggest responses in the face of these (other) problems.

However, the formulation of the arguments is contentious, in two ways worth recording: the forms of words chosen to introduce or explain key points will necessarily be contentious, sets of expressions suitable for one set of readers are less so for others. Equally, the examples used in exposition and criticism could be replaced with others; those others seeming more compelling or more persuasive to a particular readership. While problematic for any text, this is especially besetting for a text in philosophy (at least on some conceptions), where the expectation is that exactly the right form of words and exactly the right example have been selected. But what worked for one audience need not do so for another. It is a philosophical commitment here that no sense can be given to the expression "the right" in these two cases (p. 118); that both words and examples chosen represent the best I can do to make these points clearly to this imaginary audience.

Consonant with the aim to be introductory, there is no engagement with the complexities of scholarly debate: the text is written largely without the apparatus of scholarship, such as detailed quotation from sources, historical reference and the like. Instead it returns repeatedly to a number of KEY CASES, as central examples (and, to some degree, test-cases).

This text has been very long in the making. I have been thinking about the freedom of action since those undergraduate days; it provided the topic of some of my earliest publications; and I have lectured (and read papers to philosophical societies) on it for twenty years. As a result, the debts accrued are huge and, since I am probably incapable of remembering them all, let these stand for the rest: to Terry Wilkerson, my first tutor on these topics, who set me off on this line of investigation; to generations of students (especially undergraduates) at the University of Brighton, for their responses to lecture series on this topic, over the past ten years or so; to those who participated when I read papers on this topic: in particular, students at the University of Pepperdine, California, in March 1996 (and to Russ Gough for organizing the presentation), and my long-suffering students at the University of Brighton Philosophy Society, who, although asking (optimistically?) if I was going to offer a different topic this time, never appeared too disappointed at the answer; to my colleague Bob Brecher, both as stand-in for all those colleagues whose inputs I value, and for his helpful and supportive comments on a set of lectures given in Brighton in Autumn 1993; to friends who have read all or part of this text for me (even if/when I have not heeded the comments): in particular, Katherine Morris, who read all of one draft, and Gordon Baker, who read part of it. Their influence on the argument is far wider than just those places where I attribute a specific note or some such; to my wife, Myrene – although I typed this book, she contributed to every phase of its development through detailed discussion of issues and proofreading, as well as more general support.

Graham McFee
Eastbourne, February 2000

1 Free will: the issue

Introduction

Few issues in philosophy are as interesting, both to lay person and professional, as the problem of the freedom of the will (or freedom of action – the two descriptions I take to mean the same thing). For, as noted in the Preface (and as we will see), the central issue here concerns the ability to initiate (or possibility of initiating) *action*: that is, of there being (genuine) actions at all.[1] Merely being able to *will* certain actions, actions not then performed, would be indistinguishable from just wishing for impossible outcomes. And would be accommodated to the degree that such wishing itself counts as action.

Equally, over the years, few problems have seemed as intractable to philosophical solution as the problem of free action. In what follows I will both lay out the central issues involved in this philosophical problem, and consider various ways in which human concerns with freedom, responsibility and the understanding of other people are involved. Further, I shall offer (in later chapters) some thoughts on possible lines of solution. However, as a beginning, it is important to understand what the issue might be, or, more exactly, why there is an issue here at all.

Two important distinctions for understanding human activity

When we consider the world around us, and our place in it, we regularly note two related contrasts whose closer identification will take us into the question of the freedom of the will. The first distinction contrasts what might be called "agency" with what might be called "natural phenomena": roughly, a distinction between things that people *do*, as opposed to things that just occur. Consider an example. In the late 1980s (at least in England), so-called crop circles[2] – large areas in fields with crops flattened in geometrical patterns – were noted in fields of wheat, barley and the like. Two views of the origin of these crop circles offered an explanation of them as natural phenomena (although of differing sorts), while two treated them as the outcome of agency (terrestrial or extra-terrestrial).

One group attempted to explain the crop circles scientifically: for instance, invoking an electrical phenomenon (a "plasma vortex"), which might be so localized as to produce this effect. A second group talked, instead, about natural "earth forces", explained roughly like the forces evident in the phenomenon of dowsing for water, where the "natural vibrations" of the water are detected by the dowser via the hazel twig. Of course, the detail of that attempted explanation might leave it still mysterious: do we really understand dowsing for water? Are there such "earth forces" at all? Importantly, though, both these explanations represent admittedly different ways of describing the mechanism at work here: having said what the causes of the phenomenon are, the phenomenon is explained. Here the crop circles are treated as *happenings*; as naturally occurring phenomena for which no further explanation need be sought.

The third explanation offered for the crop circles was as the product of persons perpetrating some kind of hoax. Fourthly, some groups urged that the crop circles were the product of extra-terrestrial intelligences trying to contact humankind. Again, both these explanations offer – in their different ways – appropriate accounts of the crop circles in terms of *agency*: what we are told is roughly who makes them, and perhaps why.

This case shows very clearly two kinds of explanations that we standardly employ in thinking about the world around us. Some things simply happen, following through the laws of nature – in the case of crop circles, the laws of nature might be rather more complex than we presently understand, but of the same kind (say a plasma vortex, whatever that is) – or by some natural force of a different kind, as for dowsing or for ley lines, or something similar.

Equally, human beings have at least the possibility of agency – and, again, the crop circles provide a suitable model here: although the agency might be extra-terrestrial rather than human.

This distinction already raises a key question: which events should be explained in terms of agency, and which as the working out of natural processes? This may not be easy to sort out. For are not our actions as *natural* (and hence as causally explicable) as any other event?

A second distinction overlays that one, to some degree. Here, what we *do* is contrasted with things that merely *happen* to us.[3] Of course, there will be significant parallels here, since many of the things that happen to us result from natural phenomena: it rains on us as a result of . . . well, readers should fill in whatever natural laws are presently favoured by meteorologists, for example, since this represents our "best guess" as to why rainfall occurs. None the less, we standardly think of the life of humankind in terms of two varieties of occurrences. The first may reasonably be called "happenings", things that happen to us (the result of the working out of causal laws), and the second, reasonably called "actions", issue (in some way or other) from what we want or think valuable or some such. Such a conception of action may be hard to pin down more exactly: is snoring, for example, an action in this sense? But there are plenty of clear cases to concentrate on. Our standard example [KEY CASE 1] is my simply walking across the room. This will be an *action*, something I *do*, if anything is. It will be explained, perhaps, in terms of my wanting to cross the room, perhaps in terms of my crossing the room for no reason: certainly it is not the result of post-hypnotic suggestion nor of drug-taking, since either of these might raise questions about the degree to which my *not* crossing the room was "open to me" (Ginet 1990: 95). Equally, this walk across the room was not at gunpoint, nor a consequence of stress; again, cases that might seem only doubtfully actions *of mine*.

This notion of action is, to some extent, technical: in particular, it includes some omissions; cases where my failure to do something, or even my doing nothing, are relevant. So that my *not* sending my granny a Christmas card counts, for these purposes, as an action. But this is a fairly common-sense view of the scope of the idea of action: my mother might well criticize me for "what I did", where "what I did" is *fail* to send my granny the Christmas card.

However, my bodily activities, say, my walking across the room [KEY CASE 1], are also describable, using this contrast, as *happenings*. So the distinction between happenings and actions applies also to me. Then there are two ways of thinking about (describing) my behaviour: that sometimes used by my doctor, viewing me as a broken machine, as a happening; and that I would normally use of myself, where I speak in terms of what I wanted, chose, or some such: that is, I treat these events as actions.

Again, what is the basis for this distinction? Even supposing one had much more surface detail, one might well wonder whether there are patterns of explanation used exclusively on one side of the distinction, and others used exclusively on the other. Certainly, a commitment to the freedom of action must respect such distinctions.

With these two important, and common-sense, distinctions before us we can begin to move forward, clarifying what we are trying to identify in drawing such contrasts.

Responsibility, and sense of self

The distinctions just drawn are important in the understanding of our daily lives for two related reasons. First, they are integral to notions of *responsibility for one's actions*, for it seems unreasonable that anyone should be held responsible for things one could not help, things one did not choose to do and so on. That is to say, actions done from choice, for which I am morally responsible, are contrasted with events that occur without my having chosen, where I am not morally responsible. Actions done *intentionally* (for which I am morally responsible) are contrasted with events occurring not intentionally (for which I am not morally responsible, or for which my responsibility is reduced[4]). And such contrasts are enshrined in the *legal* contrast between being "fit to plead", and hence culpable (in principle), or not fit to plead and hence not culpable. Consider a very important case for us [KEY CASE 2]. the idea of *kleptomania*.[5] For our purposes, I "define" a kleptomaniac as somebody who, for instance, takes a scarf from a department store without paying for it, but who is judged to be ill (and therefore not culpable) rather than to be a thief. A kleptomaniac is not guilty of theft because he or she is not fit to plead, and that

effectively means that the "action" is not from choice or not voluntary, and hence not really an action at all. So finding this to be a case
of *kleptomania* has a clear effect in respect of responsibility: such a
person, we might say, needs to be helped or cured, rather than
punished.

Much has been written about the connection between freedom
of action, or choice, and responsibility, and I shall say something
about it later. For now, though, it is sufficient to articulate the
intuitively plausible idea that one is responsible for one's actions in
ways that one is not responsible for *mere* bodily happenings. For
example, a falling object strikes my knee in such a way as to
produce the classic "knee-jerk" reaction, sometimes used in testing
reflexes: my leg extends, knocking over a waste-paper basket. If
this is the full story, I am not responsible for the ensuing mess: it is
not my fault – the leg extension was not an action but a mere *bodily
happening*, and one obviously beyond my control.

Again, one is not responsible (or not fully responsible, perhaps)
if, for instance, one belches, so long as that belch is recognized as
resulting from gastric disorder. It is not something I chose to do, or
did deliberately, and therefore, to that degree, I am not responsible
for it. Moreover, I could not choose *not* to produce that belch
(except perhaps by careful attention to my diet): at most, I might
have delayed its emergence.[6] It is a bodily happening. Now
consider (possibly fictional) societies where belching after eating is
seen as a compliment to one's host. Then the belching would be
taken as an action, done from choice, deliberately, and so on. In *this*
case, one would be responsible for one's belching: or, more
precisely, at least for one's failure to belch.

Before beginning philosophy (at least), we think of ourselves as
clearly understanding the connection between doing something
oneself (as opposed to it merely happening) and being responsible
for that occurrence. Indeed, the word "responsible" is used in two
senses: as getting whatever praise or blame results from that action
– roughly equivalent to morally or legally responsible; and, differently, as being the agent – my being responsible for the mess might
well mean, for example, that my actions consisted in knocking over
the rubbish bin. (So this would not be the earlier case, where a
waste-paper basket's overturning was the result of a mere bodily
happening.)

Now consider a defence used by those tried for war crimes (for instance, Adolf Eichmann): "I was just obeying orders". While some orders ought not to be obeyed (as agents might decide), there is some mitigation in the fact of orders from legitimate authorities; we think of the actions as coming from the intentions or motives or whatever of those authorities.

If this connection between responsibility and choice is clear at a common-sense level, the second reason for a concern with action is rather less so. It concerns our sense of ourselves, for we think of human beings as at least sometimes *agents*, in the sense that they initiate activity. Now consider the suggestion that, instead of people around one, there were simply robots whose programming was done from some central computer. Those robots would not be performing actions at all; to be accurate, we should attribute all of their behaviour to the central programming computer. So crucial to our understanding of what does go on around us (where there are persons, not robots) is that there is agency in the world; and we, of course, are among those agents.[7] The case of the robots would be an extreme version of, say, a criminal mastermind directing his or her minions; *extreme* in the sense that these would not be minions at all, since they would simply be a step in the chain of causes by which the computer brought things about.

We note in passing how the notion of a *causal chain* arises here; a key notion for considerations of freedom of action. If B causes C and A causes B, there we are beginning to clarify the way in which C depends on A. And if A is itself the result of some earlier cause, and so on, we now have a chain stretching back, where explanation of the current event (C) will ultimately be explained in terms of some earlier event or sequence of them.[8]

In my earlier "computers and robots" story, it would be unattractive, not to say impossible, to think of oneself as such a robot. Integral to a conception of ourselves is to see us making at least some choices on some occasions. So it would be deeply problematic to give up the notions of action, choice, and such like. Giving them up would undermine not only our account of responsibility, but also our sense of ourselves. And this is the nerve of the issue concerning free will: is our common-sense understanding of ourselves as agents warranted?

What free choice is not

When considering free choice, two features can mislead us in later discussions. First, talking of "free choices" is not suggesting that one can do anything. I cannot jump over the moon: the laws of physics preclude that. As a result, I cannot choose to jump over the moon. One's choices are limited by physical possibilities of that sort, where the term "physical" here means, roughly, "explicable by the laws of physics". Equally (another case of physical [im]possibility), given my background, age and so forth, it is no longer physically possible that I become a member of the England rugby team. But my choice is limited in another important class of cases. For example, I haven't played rugby for twenty years; I'm not in relevant teams; I haven't pursued contacts with people who might know of my skills in rugby; and so forth. Or, a parallel example, having spent the past years trying to teach philosophy, the choice of becoming the managing director of a large multinational company is no longer open to me. Neither of these points, of course, says anything about the question of the freedom of action. I am "constrained" both by the laws of physics and by the "laws" of social interaction: not all possibilities are candidate choices for me.

But, now, suppose it were urged that I can *try* to, say, become managing director of the multinational company, where my (vain) efforts were taken as evidence of my so trying. Yet how is my trying in this (vain) sense more than my mere wishing? For, of course, one might well feel that this contrast exploited the borderline between two cases: I might succeed, but I don't (therefore I tried, but . . .); and I had no possibility of success (so my gestures were indicative of wishing, not trying). It may be impossible to sharply distinguish these cases in practice. But both build-in the possibility of action and choice, even when (as in the second case) that choice is severely limited.

In contrast, those who believe in the freedom of the will, or free action, are simply urging that sometimes and in some situations there are some choices open to me: that the notion of choice makes sense in this context. That is to say, they are not urging that one can always or inevitably choose anything. Indeed, one might well think that choosing one thing was always choosing *that* rather than something else; and hence that the choice was necessarily "constrained" by having to be between *this* and *that*, etc. But that is not the kind of constraint under discussion here (see note 4): rather, it is a case where the notion of choice applies. So the question (for our *determinist*: see Chapter 2, p. 21) is whether one can ever choose anything at all! I shall say more on this topic when we return to the views of those who deny that humans are agents in the relevant sense. The point here, though, is simply to recognize that defenders of free will are urging no more than that I am free to walk across rooms [KEY CASE 1], drink water and so forth, and not that I am free to become (in my earlier example) the managing director of a multinational company. So the second point is that the idea of freedom at issue in this debate is not (simply) freedom from compulsion to do this or that, but the very possibility of (genuine) action.

Notice some standard cases of non-freedom as presently under-stood; cases where one's behaviour results from physical disorder, from some drugs accidentally ingested, or from hypnosis, say. In these cases, you are not exercising choice, and so are not (usually) blamed or congratulated; or at least, the praise or blame are not as full as it might be if you were fully responsible. Here, the notion of moral responsibility doesn't really get under way. Roughly, these are physical states over which the person has no control. And kleptomania [KEY CASE 2] will provide the clearest case of occur-rences that, even at a common-sense level, are not actions, and therefore not appropriate places for moral responsibility.

As a useful comparison here, consider the following case [KEY CASE 3]. If a gunman orders me to jump out of the window or I will be shot, we may say that I have no choice. However, there is some (very limited) choice here: I can choose to jump or stand still and be shot, which I might opt for in certain circumstances (for example, if the choice involved betraying a loved one). In a contrasting situation, four burly characters seize me by my arms and legs and hurl me through the window. In that case I genuinely have no choice: in the other, a very minimal choice. For my jumping through the window at gunpoint, the notion of choice *applies*, with however small a range: for my being hurled through the window, the notion of choice simply does not apply.

Further, the notion of choice does not have application in the case of my being hurled through the window even if, at the last moment, I shout to the burly characters, "Please, please, throw me through the window!" In neither case am I *choosing*. So, cases of constraint must involve something stronger than merely cases of compulsion. As I put it before, the concern is with cases where the notion of choice does not apply.

This case allows us to see clearly (if obliquely) how what is here called "constraint" differs from "compulsion": say, the falling of stones under gravity is not compelled, although the stones' behaviour is in accordance with the causal law. Just so, if I am compelled to act in a certain way, I have a choice, albeit a limited choice (as in KEY CASE 3): the notion of choice applies to me. What is here called "constrained" behaviour (such as our kleptomaniac in KEY CASE 2) is behaviour to which the notion of choice does not apply: not actions at all. So, as KEY CASE 3 illustrates, cases of compulsion differ from cases of constraint, with our concern being with the latter.

Two "languages" for describing and explaining human events

To clarify the common-sense position, I shall introduce (in a purely technical way) a contrast between two ways of describing or explaining behaviour. I call these, with deliberate looseness, two "languages". First, in thinking of persons as agents, we are using the "language of action", of choice, of rational behaviour. This is roughly the sum of all the remarks that can be made about persons but not about inanimate objects. This point is difficult to make very precise, since (for example) both persons and rivers might run down hills. (And to distinguish different senses of the term "run" here would thereby be to concede that any contrast was not identifiable purely from the words used.) Nevertheless, such a contrast picks up our standard understanding that some characteristic ways of describing events involving humans are as human events: that is, recognizing them as *actions* rather than *happenings*, and therefore thinking of them as the result of agency rather than conceiving of them as natural phenomena.

In contrast, consider a "language of causes", of causal explanation and description. I will here take it for granted, first, that the physical sciences provide such causal descriptions and explanations, and, second, that we have a rough-and-ready understanding of such causal explanations and descriptions.

It is worth sketching some initial differences between reasons and causes. Asked why some event occurred, one variety of response (causal explanation) is in terms of some set of circumstances that, given the prevailing conditions, led to that occurrence: the response typically making an implicit or explicit reference to some scientific principle of the kind sometimes called "laws of nature". That is, asked why there was a rainstorm today, one might refer to the conditions of wind and low pressure that, at this time of year and in these latitudes, characteristically lead to rainstorms. Then saying that such conditions obtain would be explaining the occurrence of today's rainstorm: "it happened because such-and-such a weather front came in from the east". This would be to describe the cause of the rainstorm. Equally, asked why I fell forwards, you might mention the sharp blow that had been delivered between my shoulder blades: I fell because of that blow. If pressed further, you might also talk about my position at the time of the blow ("balancing on the chair") and the size of my assailant ("hit by a big bloke"). In these ways too you present a causal account of the event.

In contrast, another variety of response (reason-style explanation) might point to the agent's aim or purpose: I went on that side of the boat in order to balance it in the gust of wind, or I learned French so as to read Sartre's writings. Again, I went to Scotland for my holidays because I like the solitude, or because there is good smoked salmon and I like smoked salmon. Here, the occurrence is explained by giving reasons for its occurrence. (Notice that both kinds of explanation can begin with the word "because".) Typically, then, actions will be performed for some reason (or none), but bodily happenings will have a causal story only.

My uses of words such as "reason", "actions" and "cause" here are technical rather than everyday. So that, for example, describing the events at a peace conference typically employs the language of action. Asking, "What is the cause of the negotiations breaking down?", will, in my technical language, be a request for a *reason*. This conforms to our common-sense way of thinking about action, at least typically. Some peace conferences may break down because, say, there are no seats: more likely, though, one breaks down for the reason that the participants cannot agree who sits where.

Correspondingly, asking for the reason that my car won't start this morning is, typically, asking in the language of causes. The response is that there is water in some electrical part of the car: cars do not have *reasons* in the technical sense used here. I mention this to simplify and clarify what is said, but also to emphasize that what will be argued does not depend on a particular set of words. This is important because philosophy is often accused of being "just about words". Nothing could be further from the truth. Even in the case of our kleptomaniac [KEY CASE 2], the dispute is not whether to *call* the person a thief or a kleptomaniac, but how such a person should be treated: whether we should attempt to cure that person or to punish them.

This distinction between two languages helps to put our common-sense view more succinctly: it is that the explanation of human life requires both of these languages. For instance, my doctor thinks of my behaviour as movements of a physical body, explained causally (at least usually), and attempts to regulate the workings of this physical system, for example by giving me pills, injections and the like. Sometimes, say, in the case of mobile patients, the doctor's attitude might be mixed, regarding me as able to take the pills at a certain time, to avoid certain foods and to engage in exercise. But even then, the doctor's overall attitude is towards my body as a physical system in need of re-ordering: I am considered primarily from the causal point of view. On the other hand, in interaction with others, I see myself and them as agents, with the possibility of responsibility, and associatedly of praise and blame, for our respective actions.

"He didn't do it": three cases

So far my aim has been to articulate a common-sense view of the life of human beings and of their relationship to the physical world. Why might anyone have any reservations about the adequacy of such an account? To explore this idea, consider a set of cases where notions of *action* and of *responsibility* play a key role. In all three scenarios, the unfortunate Jones dies beneath the wheels of Smith's motor car. But did Smith do it? Was it Smith's fault? In all these cases, there is a natural tendency to suggest that Smith was *not* at fault, that he did not do it; and the cases are arranged so as to bring out a certain pattern in our thinking. These are "best case" or "most favourable case" scenarios, which means that they should be filled in with *whatever* details supplement them so as to make them most plausible.

1. [KEY CASE 4] *Smith's car is defective – some vital part of the steering mechanism has crumbled to dust, and Smith is at the wheel struggling vainly when the car passes over poor Jones.*

   This is a "best case" scenario, so let the defectiveness be something the driver could not spot, and let him have done whatever are reasonable checks on the car. Indeed, let him have done checking to the *n*th degree, so that he had the car serviced by professionals that very morning, but this was a peculiar kind of undetectable metal fatigue, say.

   Here Smith had done all he could, and perhaps more than most of us would (or we do), to ensure the car's roadworthiness. Surely Smith is not responsible in this case: he just didn't do it. Roughly, the causes of the event were elsewhere. There is mechanical causation at work here: so that Smith's acts become irrelevant at a certain point. He is no longer in control of the car: he couldn't help it.

2. [KEY CASE 5] *Poor Smith has a heart attack while he a driving, and is paralysed. Then the car runs over the unlucky Jones.*

   Again, this is a "best case" scenario, so let Smith have had all the normal check-ups including visiting an eminent heart specialist that very morning. But this was an undetectable heart condition.

   Here again, surely Smith was not responsible – he didn't do it – because there was/is an explanation in terms of causes beyond Smith's control, although now they amount to events within Smith's body.

3. [KEY CASE 6] *Smith had a tumour pressing (or whatever) on his brain, and so steers the car in a straight line on a certain bend, and hence over the unfortunate Jones.*

   Again, since this is a "best case" scenario, let Smith have recently undergone whatever tests you like, but let this condition be an undetectable one. This resembles the second case, except that now the cause is in the brain of Smith. (And this will be important in what follows, since causality involving the brain is the norm.) Here again Smith didn't do it; the death of Jones did not issue from a wish or from a desire (or even a whim) of Smith's. Like the other cases, this is surely an accident: something no doubt regrettable, but really no one's fault.

The moral from these three cases is that, with events in which a persons is involved but not *doing* the thing in question (as Smith didn't really do it in these three cases), then they are not responsible for that event. The person is not being a moral agent in respect of that event. In the case of real accidents, there are no such agents.

All this follows from the fact that, in each of these scenarios, the event was caused by (roughly) something other than Smith, even though in the second and third cases that "something" was inside Smith or a part of Smith. These cases show how a kind of explanation (in terms of causes), that is characteristically used in the natural sciences, may be applied to human beings, or to human activity.

In all these cases, Smith is not culpable (or not fully culpable). But our easy explanation – "matters beyond Smith's control", say – simply will not work when the "matters" at issue derive from states of Smith's body. For, on the face of it, all the events for which Smith *is* responsible derive, at least mediately, from states within his body. Still, the direction of thought suggested by these cases should be clear enough.

Notice, first, that we can imagine the ensuing courtroom battle in which the defence attorneys argue that what occurred was not murder; while the prosecution urges that it was. Here the dispute is whether to characterize the event as one in which the driver Smith was an active agent, and hence murdered Jones, or to say that the driver was not an active agent, was not acting deliberately or intentionally: that to some degree, and perhaps wholly, this is something which simply occurred. While it is a discussion of what to say (or how to characterize the event), its implications are profound: was it murder or something else . . . say, (only) manslaughter? To opt for this later sort of account is to focus on descriptions of the event in terms of the language of causes: that is to say, to focus on, at best, the movements of the body solely, ceasing to regard the event as the action of some person. What I am calling *movements of the body* are explained and described in the same way as movements of other physical events in the universe: that is, they are described and explained by talking (either formally or informally) in the sorts of (causal) terms characteristic of science.

Second, at least some of these cases, as I have described them, are clear examples of constraint, rather like that of our kleptomaniac [KEY CASE 2]. Often Smith, like the kleptomaniac, is not really an agent here. These are cases where it is very natural to accept that the person is not responsible for what occurs: he or she did not really do it. And here, ceasing to characterize an event as an action of the person removes at least some of the responsibility at issue. For only events characterized as actions are things people *do*, as opposed to things that just occur. So there is a clear connection between questions of morality and the common-sense idea of people as free agents. If we cannot describe events as "actions", we cannot offer praise or blame (or any other moral comment) on anything that occurs; it would be like, say, blaming a snooker ball or a planet. For what is explained via "laws of nature", as "naturally occurring", is not amenable to moral judgement; earthquakes, no matter how destructive, cannot be morally evil, any more than (say) the falling rain is.

Finally, notice (at least parenthetically) the increasing tendency to use description in the language of causes; say, in respect of the doings of so-called "juvenile delinquents", seen as products of under-privilege, poverty and the like. This causal story is presented to explain their not being fully culpable. Such people are seen, like kleptomaniacs, as in need of help or cure, rather than punishment, at least to some degree (Flew 1973: Pt III). The structure of such an argument is that if the person's behaviour is appropriately considered causally (or to the degree that it is so considered), then it does not constitute *action*, is not suitable for praise, blame or the ascription of responsibility.

It should be clear by now how our common-sense understanding of persons and action might be argued against, by urging the primacy of the language of causes. Opponents would take the causal descriptions as primary and urge that descriptions and explanations that mention choosing and deciding (and so on) involve some kind of conceptual confusion. At its heart, this position simply involves treating all behaviour by human beings in the way that the rest of us treat the kleptomaniac and the unfortunate Smith [KEY CASES 4–6]. The central thought, to which I return (Chapters 2 and 3), is that what humans do can be explained, or at least described, using remarks from the "hard sciences": in particular, biophysics and biomechanics. Such remarks do no justice to the sorts of reasons normally offered for human action. In short, they will be causal descriptions and explanations. We call adherents of such a view "determinists". And here, in line with comments in Chapter 2,[9] we will reserve this term for those who regard the "ordinary" action-type explanations as empty.

Such determinists allow that human actions are, in principle, *predictable* in roughly the ways other phenomena are predictable,[10] via the causal laws that govern them. For example, we can predict a rainstorm by noting that rainstorms occur under such-and-such conditions, and that those conditions now obtain in London. Hence, other things being equal, it is now raining in London. This follows from the causal laws governing rainstorms, together with the prevailing conditions. I shall elaborate this argument in Chapter 2. But notice that "predictability in principle" here does not require that actual prediction be done nor that it could presently be done: it is logically independent of such actual predicting. For we may well know neither the causal laws nor the current conditions. If the movement of the planets [KEY CASE 7] is now the subject for accurate prediction (the argument would run), it was always predictable, whether or not people were able to do the predicting (whether they had the technology). So whether or not there was actual predicting is beside the point. To clarify, the words "predict" and "prediction" here are used as in natural sciences and not as in fortune telling or any kind of guessing. To continue the planetary motion example, predicting the motion of Mars, or the eclipses of the moon, is not just guessing: an understanding of the laws of physics guarantees that the predictions will be true, at least in so far as those laws and theories are trustworthy. I shall say more about these ideas in Chapter 2.

Fatalism

It is worth putting aside, even at this early stage, a particular view, sometimes called "fatalism", that the last couple of paragraphs may have suggested: the view that, since events are determined, activity is pointless. A good example occurs in Goncharov's play *Oblomov*, where the central character simply stays in bed all the time, judging that, since all events are determined, there is nothing he can do. So nothing is worth getting up for: he might as well stay in bed.

But Oblomov's position is not of a piece with those we are considering. If he can genuinely decide to stay in bed, he can make decisions: the notion of choice still applies to him. His explanation of his behaviour continues to employ the language of action. Of course, his choices may be severely limited. Like many of us, he may no longer aspire to manage a multinational company. Indeed, given his current financial situation, his prospects of improving that situation, and the costs of all the activities he finds pleasurable, he may prefer to stay in bed. But this is a choice, just one from a limited range. (And perhaps we could point him to cheaper pleasures, etc.)

The impossibility of genuine fatalism of this kind is amusingly illustrated in a story by Somerset Maugham (van Inwagen 1983: 24: Thornton 1989: 62). Here, a servant, having met Death in a market place and received a strange look from her, has feared for his imminent demise, borrowed a horse from his master and fled to another city. The master later has a conversation with Death in which she explains that the look she gave the servant was one of surprise: she had a date that evening with the servant and was surprised to see him here, the date being for the very far off city whence the servant had fled! The point, of course, is that had the servant done nothing, stayed put, he would have avoided death (or Death). In so far as the servant was free to choose whether or not to flee to the distant city, he was a free agent, and fatalism is false. His death could have been avoided.

There is, however, another way to think of such cases, not merely fatalistically. In so far as we think his death inevitable, we think that his choosing to flee to another city was constrained in the strong sense discussed earlier. That is, the servant only appeared to have a choice here. The servant's flight was the inevitable event: he was *bound* to see Death, to pursue his master to lend him the horse, and so on. So he did not really choose these things at all (despite appearing to). In this case, it makes no sense to argue one might as well do *nothing*. For whether or not one "did" anything would not be a matter for one's own decision. Like the servant in the story, how one was going to behave would be inevitable. If these considerations were correct, one could not *do* anything; the notion of action does not apply and the language of action is some kind of sham. But that position is much stronger than the sort of fatalism characteristic of, say, Oblomov.

In terms of the earlier distinction (p. 9), fatalism presents issues of constraint as though they concerned compulsion: as though

Death could compel the servant to be in such-and-such a place. But the determinist will rather argue (Chapter 2, p. 21) for constraint; cases where the notion of choice does not apply.

Conclusion

In this chapter, I have presented a common-sense understanding of persons and of action, arguing that action was fundamental both to our sense of ourselves and to the possibility of moral agency, with its associated responsibility. Will this account of ourselves and others survive criticism based on other explanations we want to give? In particular, are we really so different from the unfortunate Smith (in the cases above) who did not count as an agent? For this is the centre of the worry here: although common-sense assures us that we are not robots, can we really demonstrate that fact? I have begun to introduce views of those who might seek to deny the common-sense conclusion – as we will see in Chapter 2, these are *determinists* – and I have attempted to avoid the confusion that consideration of fatalism might introduce.

But is human activity not on a par with other events in the universe? And, if so, is it not plain arrogance to imagine that humans are not part of the same causal system as everything else? Yet it seems that we typically do this. A suitable way of posing this issue asks: does it make sense to distinguish some events involving humans (as actions) from the rest of what goes on (happenings)? The remaining chapters attempt to grapple with this issue.

It is worth adding that one should present one's opponent's views in their strongest case rather than their weakest. This is a general principle in philosophy: that, before critically addressing an opponent's position, one makes that position as strong as possible, supplementing and reconstructing where necessary; further, that one gives the benefit of the doubt where this seems required. Applied to our case, it means that we must consider opposition to uses of the language of action where that opposition depends on what one might call a *minimal physicalism*. Thus, one should concede that human beings are composed of flesh, bone and such like; and that these are in turn composed of molecules, atoms and whatever smaller pieces science discovers for us. It seems unproductive to appeal, in these arguments, to insubstantial notions (for example, to souls).

First, and least important, the introduction of non-material "entities" raises at least as many problems as it solves. As an example, consider positions often ascribed to Descartes, on which persons were viewed as having a body in a physical realm, with physical properties, and a mind in a psychical or mental realm, with wholly mental properties. Of course, such a view readily generates the freedom of the *will*. For the psychical realm is, by definition, not constrained by the laws of science. The sorts of constraint we have been describing have no application in that situation. Descartes' problem, though, (on this view) is to explain free *action*. For he must go on to explain how this non-physical "thing" can effect the physical: how my thoughts about digging the garden can be related to my picking up the shovel, and so forth. I will not expand these points here, since this is the topic of much philosophical writing.[11] Notice, though, that such a view can scarcely offer an attractive solution to any doubts raised about the viability of the language of action: it will be difficult to connect activity in such a psychical realm to the everyday behaviours of drinking glasses of water, walking across rooms [KEY CASE 1] and such like.

A second difficulty is that such a position effectively begs the question[12]: if action is essentially to be understood in terms of events in such a psychical realm, then any conflict between thinking of actions of persons in terms of science and thinking of them in other ways will, while the events are conceived as occurring in the physical world, always be beside the point. Thus, to give our opponent the strongest possible case, we should concede the assumption of *minimal physicalism*. As we will see, this assumption will take us even further, leading us to consider physical determinism – a topic for later chapters.

2 Determinism: exposition

Introduction

In Chapter 1 we saw how a common-sense account of the life and activity of human beings builds in the conception of humans as free agents. How might that position be attacked or undermined? Chapter 1 identified the protagonist of such an attack as the determinist: but what precisely is his or her position? As the term is used here, a *determinist* disputes the viability of the contrasts mentioned in Chapter 1: he urges that the language of action is based on the contrasts identified there (pp. 1–4), contrasts that prove (on investigation) to be spurious. But why should someone believe that such seemingly fundamental contrasts, say, between someone *doing* something and something happening to one, were actually spurious? Our first task must be to articulate the determinist position as persuasively as we can.

The central thought is that what humans do can be explained, or at least described, using remarks from the "hard sciences", as we noted in Chapter 1. As a result, what humans do will have the same kind of predictability (in principle) as other happenings have, although perhaps of greater complexity. The interest of determinism lies in its offering the view that (on account of the predictability in principle of human behaviour) all talk of choosing to do this or that is, on investigation, mistaken or misguided. That is to say, the determinist urges that human behaviour could be described solely in causal terms (perhaps in terms of movement of the body): and, moreover, it should be described in those sorts of ways if we are to be consistent. The determinist points out that even non-determinists do not think that the behaviour of kleptomaniacs [KEY CASE 2] involves choice, nor that of persons with certain sorts of brain tumour [KEY CASE 6]. We say, "they can't help it", and treat their (seeming) "actions" as caused by the disease or whatever. These are the familiar cases of constraint, from Chapter 1. The determinist merely urges that all human behaviour is caused in exactly this sense. So that, if these cases are appropriately described in causal terms, all cases of human behaviour should be.

Recall three points made earlier. First, the distinction between predictability *in principle* and actual prediction: to recognize that a certain event is predictable in principle does not suggest that prediction could actually be done. No doubt there was a time when prediction of the motion of planets [KEY CASE 7] was in practice impossible; nevertheless, the movements of the planets were predictable, because they were predictable in principle. So that viewing human behaviour as predictable is not equivalent to thinking that we can *do* the prediction. On the contrary, a central claim of determinists is that our current state of predictive power is logically irrelevant.

Second, the word "predict" is not equivalent to "guess". As in the case of planetary motion, prediction here amounts to working out what will occur at some future time rather than estimating as a forecaster might. So, talking of prediction here is more a guarantee than a surmise.

Third, the inexorability central to such cases contrasts the choice (however limited) of the person ordered to jump through a window at gunpoint with the case of the person thrown from the window [KEY CASE 3]. In only the second situation is the behaviour determined in the relevant sense. So that the opponent of free will, the determinist, is not asking whether one has a choice or not. In many cases, one may have little or no choice: in the example, the "choice" is to be dead from gunshot wounds in the room, or from a broken back (from the fall) outside. Rather, the determinist questions whether or not the notion of choice has any application. Now, even non-determinists contrast *some* cases that are causally explicable with cases where choice applies. The determinist concludes that, since all human behaviour is causally explicable, the notion of action has no application to the "behaviour" of human beings, as it does not to the "behaviour" of, say, stones falling under gravity.

With these background remarks in place, we can present our determinist position more formally.

The determinist argument

In terms of what comes later, it will be useful to have some fairly formal exposition of the argument of our determinist. Such an argument might be given in six steps, as follows:

1. Every event has a cause (as science tends to show).
2. Actions are a kind of event.
3. Therefore every action has a cause (from 1 and 2 above).
4. Therefore every action which actually is performed has to be performed, given the antecedent state of the world (the "cause" in premise 3): that is, there is causal necessity.
5. Therefore it makes no sense to talk of "choosing" to do this or that. For, given the causal antecedents (that is, the antecedent state of the world), we could not do otherwise than we do. We are governed by causal necessity.
6. Therefore explaining events in terms of reasons, which depends on the notion of people choosing to do this or that, can be discarded as empty.

In succeeding sections, I will comment on each premise in turn. (And, remember, this is our attempt to present a plausible determinism: later chapters will explore reasons for doubting or disputing these premises.) But, first, there is no standard use of the term "determinism".[1] However, the argument put forward above characterizes a *determinist* position in the sense in which that word is used here: it begins from the idea of universal causation and concludes that the language of action can be discarded as vacuous, implying that there can be no such thing as responsibility. There is a terminological decision here (recorded previously): some writers use the term "determinist" only for those who accept the first premise of my determinist argument: that is, accept that every event has a cause. Readers will not be confused as long as they recognize that this is a terminological matter only; and that some name must be found for those who reach the conclusion of this argument.[2] So, here, *determinism* is the thesis that there are (in reality) no such things as genuine choices – that the language of choice is spurious – where this follows from universal causation (appropriately understood). So that a commitment to (the truth of) "every event has a cause" does not, of itself, make one a determinist: one must further urge that *therefore* choice is illusory.

Also, this is the barest outline of an argument for determinism, to be given substantial content in a number of different ways. In the seventeenth and eighteenth centuries, humans were typically modelled as physical mechanisms with (figuratively) internal wires and pulleys. In the twentieth century, a biomechanical model of humankind is often used, which is a long way from the wires-and-pulleys model of one thing causing another. Thus the complexity of the determinist argument may be concealed in this simple exposition of it. None the less, this argument should be filled-in in whatever ways make it most powerful; and we will see later what those might be.

However, we should always seek the strongest version of opponents' arguments. Presenting the determinist position in as powerful a form as we can will involve taking on board (temporarily) certain ideas seen from a determinist perspective: for instance, the conception of "predictability in principle" (see pp. 15, 20). But these are ideas we will want to re-evaluate later. So adopting them here must be *for the sake of the argument*; as ideas to think about, rather than simply accept. Further, we should expect of the determinist some reason to adopt that idea, and some understanding of it. In this case, the determinist does both by appeal to a central example [KEY CASE 7]: the movement of a particular planet was governed by a causal law at a particular time, since it was always governed by that law, but people at that time did not know the law. An occurrence (the planet's movement) was always predictable, it seems plausible to believe – after all, it is predictable now – but our attention is directed to a time when the prediction could not be made: then, the event was not predictable in practice. But, since it was predictable, it must have been predictable in *principle*. This is then offered as a model for the kind of predictability the determinist deals in. In this way, the determinist both motivates the idea of events predictable in principle and explains that idea to us.

Additionally, this exposition of determinism is not perfect: not all the premises have the same status. But by making clearer the bases on which such determinism might stand, a formal exposition will help us when we come to consider how determinism might be combated (with later chapters disputing each of these premises). We must now turn to the clarification of the argument.

Science, laws and truth

At first glance, premise 1 appears to be an empirical claim, as though someone had investigated events and found them all to have causes. So it can seem like a discovery, say, of natural science, that "every event has a cause".[3] Yet this is not so. Rather, the claim that every event has a cause is a basic commitment of natural science; something from which science begins, rather than something discovered (see below). So premise 1 states an assumption of the project of modern science: that, in principle, causal laws explaining the occurrence of a particular event may be sought, seeing that event as the result of an antecedent state of affairs.

We should, for these purposes, treat the causal laws, which might be called "the laws of nature", as true; that is, not concern ourselves with complexities about their precise status as laws. Many of what we now take to be laws of nature, as described by physics, are in actuality false: but this does not undermine our commitment to such laws. In fact, it is just another way of saying that we do not yet know what the laws of nature really are (Feynman 1992 [1965]: 33).

This premise seems quite plausible: we should not readily give it up. For instance, consider some apparently mysterious event, say, in the Bermuda Triangle. Although presently puzzled as to why aeroplanes and ships should disappear over and in this particular region of the sea, our commitment is to there being some kind of explanation here, and that, if this is indeed a natural phenomenon, the explanation will be a causal one of the kind available in science. Perhaps it may use notions not presently available in science, but that, again, is another way of acknowledging that science may progress. At least initially,[4] then, premise 1 of the determinist argument is powerful and appealing, certainly more appealing than its denial.

Additionally, the idea of every event having a cause is, I am suggesting, part of the project of science: nothing here depends on science actually having discovered such causes to date. Further, the place of science is not, strictly, part of the argument, but it is the basis on which we will (temporarily) be accepting and arguing for premise 1.

Actions, events and causality

In turning to other premises, remember that our aim is to make a persuasive case for later consideration. Seen this way, premise 2 asserts, simply, that actions are a kind of event. This premise should be taken together with premise 3, which draws the conclusion that every action has a cause. Since human beings are made of the same "bits" – atoms, molecules, sub-atomic particles, etc. – as constitute other things around us, the movements of my body are as much events as the movement of clouds, for example. Both consist simply in the motion of these "bits" (at whatever level of complexity) and can be explained in terms of whatever scientific laws govern them. Thus the "bodily motions" comprising the *action* constitute an event (premise 2). Then, if actions are a type of event, and every event has a cause (premise 1), it will follow that every action has a cause. Of course, all we are acknowledging is that, since human beings are composed of the same atoms, etc. as the rest of the universe, they too will be subject to causal laws of just the same sort, although perhaps of a greater complexity. Yet complexity as such is not the issue. As with predicting planetary motion [KEY CASE 7], complexity may preclude prediction in practice, but what is predictable in principle is, for that reason, predictable. And mere complexity (although making prediction in practice very difficult) will not preclude, in principle, predictability.

A practical objection here urges that the complexity of the task precludes its fulfilment: "our evil scientists will be swamped by *combinatorial explosion*" (Dennett 1991: 5, original emphasis). But this confuses the practical problem with the philosophical one: rather like the case of planetary motion before the discovery of relevant "covering" laws [KEY CASE 7], the possibility here is realized since what is predictable in principle is, therefore, predictable.[5]

So there is no obvious problem here: if causal laws apply at all, it seems that these two premises too should be accepted. At first blush, each seems more plausible than its denial.

Premise 4 stands in need of most explanation. The central idea, *causal necessity*, comes to this: under those very conditions that a determinist would regard as determining a particular event, no other event could have happened. A simple example [**KEY CASE 8**] explains. Given the laws of physics and the composition of billiard balls and billiard table, any bits of dust on the table and so on, when moving ball *A* comes into contact with stationary ball *B*, this second ball will move off with a certain speed and direction. And it is necessary, given the relevant laws and the initial conditions, that ball *B* should move off in just that way.

Of course, the laws might break down. The "necessity" is conditional on those laws. But if they break down, they were not really laws in the first place, and scientists will look for other causal laws. Given the laws, the resultant movement of ball *B* is necessary, as are its speed and direction. Here we see *causal necessity* in operation. Causal necessity, for the determinist, means that only one set of outcomes is possible, given the initial situation: the past determines a unique future. Suppose instead that, under that set of initial conditions, one of two events, either event *E* (the second ball moves off) or event *F* (both balls remain still), could have happened, and event *E* did happen. Then either no explanation could be given why *E* rather than *F* took place (which is crazy – surely there must be an explanation for this rather than that happening), or else the set of initial conditions need to be supplemented in some way so as to now explain why *F* did not happen and *E* did. Suppose a billiard player plays a particular shot, potting a particular ball on one occasion; then, on another occasion when the balls are in the same position, plays the same shot but fails to pot the ball. What must we say? We must conclude that, contrary to appearances, the situations were not exactly equivalent. Perhaps the balls were not in precisely the same position. Perhaps he did not cue with exactly the same "weight" or direction. Perhaps there was dust on the table or chalk on the balls, or some such. All in all, there *must* have been some such difference since, had there been no difference in those initial conditions, the same outcome would have resulted. That is to say, causal necessity gives the view that, for whatever happens, there prevail conditions under which nothing else could happen; and therefore that whatever actually happens had to happen, given conditions at that time.

Yet the picture is not complete enough yet. Unforeseen circumstances can upset the apple cart. If the legs on the billiard table suddenly give way, or the table is struck by a meteorite, one would expect different outcomes than those predicted. So the statement of initial conditions must cover all such possibilities. Hence it describes a state of the universe at a particular time, which, given the causal laws, leads to a new state of the universe at a succeeding time, say, a split second later (compare van Inwagen 1982: 47). In this way, premise 4 is an "unpacking" of what it means to speak of one event as causing another; and emphasising the importance (within that idea) of causal necessity. Indeed, one aspect of the notion "cause" is its compelling in this way (see Flew 1986: 81–2).

Recall, too, the idea of a *causal chain* (p. 4). A first event, the movement of billiard ball *A*, causes the second, the movement of billiard ball *B*, yet that first event is itself caused (the product of earlier events, governed by causal laws and initial conditions). And whatever caused the movement of billiard ball *A* is itself an event with a cause, and so on further back. So, although we describe just one link in this chain of causes, the picture picks out the ramifying chain of such causes.

We can (and do) take causes as necessitating in the ways described above. This suggests that premise 4 too should be adopted (at least initially: this conception of causal necessity will be re-examined in Chapter 8). Indeed, our everyday conception of causation has, at its heart, the idea that, if two outcomes differ, there must be a prior difference, in either the initial situation or in which are the relevant causal laws. And this is just what we have been emphasizing.

Premise 5 of our determinist argument is just an amplification of this picture of causal necessity from premise 4. The determinist simply urges that all changes in human bodies, or brought about by human bodies, are as much the result of the causal laws as the changes (in position and velocity) of one billiard ball brought about by another. If accepted, this conclusion would have, as an outcome, that the notion of choice is a fraudulent one: people no more choose than do billiard balls. Premise 6 states just this conclusion.

Further, this account of the determinist's position builds in its incompatibility with genuine ("free") action: in this way, the conclusion is substantive – that the concept of action has no application to human behaviour.[6]

This argument does not depend on any particular set of causal laws. It is wholly general: exactly the same argument (with only minor modification) could be filled in using biochemical causes, where the units of causation might be sub-atomic particles, or psychological causes, or mechanical causes. The crucial element here is really in premise 4: as long as the idea of causation can be unpacked to give *causal necessity*, we have an appropriate formulation of the argument for determinism, although, as we will see, there are practical reasons for selecting one kind of determinism for our consideration. Nevertheless, this is one reason why it is not necessary to be concerned with finding a completely acceptable formulation of the determinist's argument: that is to say, with worrying about precise formulation (see also Chapter 3). As it stands, this argument is relatively well-formed:[7] that most premises represent a kind of unpacking of the previous one, in a way makes the argument compelling.

Finally, notice how powerful this argument is. Were it accepted, it would have the consequence that, since people's actions are governed by the same causal laws as the "actions" of (for example) billiard balls, we have no reason for praising, blaming, holding responsible (etc.) people, and not doing the same for billiard balls. And since we are not tempted by freedom or responsibility for billiard balls,[8] we should not be tempted by those ideas for human beings. The difference, according to this view, is only one of complexity. Of course the determinist accepts that we cannot make predictions about human behaviour, given our present level of technology, but his or her model may be likened to that of an aerial view of railway sidings. From far up, we may be unable to predict the movements of the trains, and our equipment may never be accurate enough to allow us to see the rails. Nevertheless, the trains are following the rails exactly.

What kind of determinism?

If this is our determinist position, expressed via the argument above (p. 21), is there any reason for understanding the causation in one way rather than another? In Chapter 1, the point was made that an opponent's argument should be confronted in its strongest form: does this give us a reason for treating the causation in one way rather than another? There is, I would urge, just such a reason, which leads us to consider the causation as operating at a level described by natural science, and perhaps ultimately by physics. This turns on the plausibility of attributing *causal necessity*. As we will see (Chapter 3, p. 50), on alternative versions, the notion of causal necessity seems less convincing than when the causes are interpreted along lines suggested by physical sciences. With that in mind, I shall adopt the view that, from now on, the notion of a cause will be thought of in this way. Hence the determinism will be physical determinism;[9] the causal laws under consideration will be those described by the hard sciences (perhaps ultimately by physics).

This is also the right choice to get the strongest form of determinism in place since science seems to be offering the ultimate description of events, picking out the ultimate causation:[10] whatever is explained in some other way for some practical human purposes, say, in terms of one's psychology, or of economic forces, must rest in the end on descriptions of one's behaviour in terms of the movements of one's anatomy and physiology, matters addressed by our science.

However, such accounts of behaviour will very often require a causal chain leading back to changes in one's brain and central nervous system, and of course beyond that. So the causes may be seen as operating outwards from the brain and central nervous system, although in reality that will be one link in a longer causal chain. Further, even though our concern is with physical determinism, a helpful shorthand will describe events at a more common-sense level. So, speaking about, say, my musculature may be a useful shorthand, while acknowledging that changes in musculature may be explained as part of a longer causal chain, and perhaps would be better described as changes at a molecular level.

Causality – some further remarks

It may be useful to draw together some of the remarks on causal explanation as we have been developing the idea thus far, both in this chapter and earlier (Chapter 1, p. 9). (This summary is slightly more technical than other parts of the chapter, and so might be skip-read.)

First, a central idea, for our understanding of the world around us, is of *causal regularity*: we depend on the fact that, if a set of circumstances A led to an outcome B yesterday, and if nothing else relevant is different, then A will lead to B today, too. In this sense, causality is the cement of the universe;[11] its uniformity is presupposed in explanation in general and in scientific explanation in particular. This stresses the externality of laws of nature (causal laws): as Bird puts it, "Laws are the things in the world which we try to discover" (1998: 26). For this reason, our response to the determinist argument should resist "playing fast and loose" with the analysis of causality.

Second, causal laws have the form of subjunctive conditionals, and also of counterfactual conditionals (Carruthers 1992: 43): that is to say (respectively), they take the form:

- *If* X *were to be* the case, then Y would be the case. (Subjunctive.)
- If X had been the case, Y *would have been* the case. (Counterfactual.)

Taken together, these amount to saying that, when A caused B, B would not have happened (on this occasion) if A had not happened. Further, if (in sufficiently similar circumstances) an event of kind A were to happen in the future, then an event of kind B would happen also.

Third, such causal explanations are regularly found in natural sciences; for example, in physics. For there too we are looking at events where, if A were to happen, B would too; and if C had not happened, D would not have.

Taken together, these ideas tie the concept of a cause into the sorts of regularity treated as "laws of nature", and lead naturally to a conception of *causal necessity*: the occurrence of one kind of event (A) makes the subsequent occurrence of any other kind of event (than B) a physical impossibility. Now, this is a very natural way to read the common-sense picture of causality sketched here: if later we choose to deny it, we must see our view as revisionary of quite a lot of everyday thinking.

Finally, consider a so-called Humean conception of causation,[12] which recognizes that our observation of causes at work is really just the observation of one event (or one kind of event) being regularly followed by another event (or kind of event): that we never observe the "must" in operation, even though we predict the occurrence of the second kind of event when we see the first ("the water has frozen in these copper pipes so they will burst"). For Hume, then, causation was no more than "constant conjunction" of one kind of event with another, with a temporal priority to one (the cause precedes the effect) and with a spatial connection between them. But, of course, this analysis still permits (in principle) the drafting of the same causal laws, interpreted in terms of causal necessity, for it insists that the "conjunctions" of cause and effect be "constant"!

So this picture of causality might be elaborated in these ways. As we have seen, its heart lies in the view of causes as necessitating, or of causal necessity.

How not to object to determinism

If this is the account of determinism under consideration, it is worth noting three inappropriate lines of objection. The first invokes the feeling of choosing to do this or that, in order to combat the determinist. Yet one cannot simply say, "But I know that I am choosing". For here the determinist reminds us of cases, like that of the kleptomaniac [KEY CASE 2], where even believers in free will accepted that the notion of choice did not apply. Yet the kleptomaniac may well think or feel that he or she is choosing to act in such a way. So what one thinks or feels here cannot make a logical difference. Also, one does not generally feel free or otherwise when one performs everyday actions. No doubt I sometimes listen to the car straining up the hill and decide whether or not to change gear; but usually the slightest sound of the engine labouring precipitates action. There is no "feeling" of choice in the second case, one way or the other, despite it being a typical case of what non-determinists would call a free action. This example simply shows that appeals to feeling free or seeming free are simply beside the point: the question is whether one *is* free, whether the notion of choice has any application here. And the determinist's argument suggests to us that it does not.

A second inappropriate way of arguing against determinism will urge, contrary to assumptions made here, that the human actions must be understood as involving some non-physical element, such as a mind, soul or spirit. This view, sometimes called *dualism* and associated with Descartes, is clearly inappropriate. For how could the mental or psychological event "propel" the physical one? Clearly, it could not, in its own terms.

As we saw in Chapter 1, the advocate of dualism must explain how the initiation of action is possible, given that our bodies are composed of atoms and smaller particles, and hence obey causal laws appropriate to such physical objects. There do not seem to be breaks in our chains of causes, so this is impossible. Thus, a commitment to the physicality of human beings seems crucial. There are no non-physical "parts" of persons: at the least, such a view would require adherence to one of two bizarre views.

With the first view, the non-physical parts none the less enter into causal relations with the physical parts.[13] But to enter into causal relations with the physical is a pretty good account of what being *physical* consists in: for, say, to exert pressure on some physical object seems to require another physical object – a shadow could not do it! The alternative position is that, despite not entering into causal relations, the non-physical nevertheless shapes the movement of the physical. Yet how can this be? What sense can be given to the term "shapes"? If the movements of a person's limbs follow the causal patterns, and are determined in that way, there seems no room for any other type of account of human activity: the behaviour seems fully explained. So one cannot simply deny determinist conclusions in this way.

A third misguided way to object to determinism picks up the connection, voiced here, between determinism and predictability. Thus the objector might urge that events are not predictable, since we cannot predict them. But this is simply to confuse actual prediction with what the determinist requires: predictability in principle.

These three considerations illustrate aspects of the strength of the determinist position: it cannot simply be put aside with platitudes about our *knowing* (or, worse, feeling) that we are free agents. Rather, determinism represents a philosophical challenge to such ideas, and does so because it draws on our common-sense commitments to explanation (by science) of events in the world around us. And one aspect of such commitment will be to the "materiality" or "physicality" of human beings: that we are continuous with the rest of the natural world.

Of course, the challenge of determinism might be met in a number of different ways (and we will be surveying some of them in later chapters): so it is useful to have a name for the opponent of determinism, neutral between the many positive theses such a person might hold. Therefore I speak here of "the free will defender", who asserts that notions of choice etc. do (at least on some occasions) apply in respect of human behaviour.

Determinism and responsibility

The claims of the determinist obviously conflict with our everyday notion of humans as morally responsible, as responsible for their actions. The determinist begins by reminding us (free will defenders) of cases where we too accept that, when behaviour is found to be caused, notions of moral responsibility do not apply. In the case of the kleptomaniac [KEY CASE 2], the free will defender concludes that, because the kleptomaniac could not do otherwise than take the scarf from the department store, he or she is not responsible: there is no free agent here, nor is this a free action. These are our distinctions between actions done intentionally and actions not done intentionally, enshrined in the legal contrast between being fit to plead (and hence culpable) or not fit to plead (and hence not culpable: Chapter 1, p. 4).

The determinist then urges that his or her argument (p. 21) illustrates that all human behaviour is causally determined in just the way that the kleptomaniac's behaviour is. He or she reminds us, again, of cases [KEY CASES 4–6] where we are happy to say "he didn't do it" and therefore absolved Smith of responsibility in the death of the unfortunate Jones (or mitigated that responsibility): the determinist's point is that all behaviour is causally determined in just the way our cases there were. To put the matter vividly, we are all robots in precisely that way.

This amounts, of course, to an assertion of an incompatibility between determinism and (moral) responsibility. Indeed, that is precisely the outcome of the determinist argument (p. 21): for the determinist there urges that the language of action is based on spurious contrasts, and hence has no application for human behaviour. If this point is accepted, and granting the connection of morality to choice, it follows that the notion of (moral) responsibility is an empty one.

Who are such determinists? A comprehensive discussion of determinism is relevant both for those accused, in different ways, of being determinists (for instance, Freud and Marx[14]) and to those (apparently) committed to a deterministic conception of human kind: for instance, if computers are fully deterministic (and they must be, for how else could we rely on them?), anyone who models human mental activity in terms of the activity of computers seems to be conceptualizing human mental activity deterministically. Members of either group might subsequently show that they were not determinists after all or that their determinism did not constitute an objection to (or a difficulty for) their position, but all should welcome the investigation! And if they do not, *we* should see it as one aspect of an interrogation of such a position.

Some oddities of being a determinist

It is worth recording, at this stage, three oddities in being a determinist, flagging peculiarities. First, for the determinist, only causal explanation is required to explain human behaviour. But his or her argument involves notions such as *necessity*, *possibility* and *inevitability*: it claims that certain things "must" happen, and such like. Yet the determinist has offered no way to "read" such notions in causal terms. Nor is it clear how one would go about doing so.

Second, some of the attraction of determinism comes from a "wires-and-pulleys" notion of causes. If causes are not like that, some of the attractiveness of the position may disappear. However, this point should not be overstated. So long as an intelligible notion of cause is in operation (for example in physics) and that notion is interpreted so as to produce causal necessity (see p. 24), the determinist position is not really undermined.

Third, it can be a thankless task being a determinist. For, as we saw above, there is no suitable way for a determinist to describe being a determinist except in causal terms. You cannot say, for example, "I chose to be a determinist as the most rational view", since neither the notion of *rationality* nor of *choice* are causal notions. As an illustrative example: I once heard a philosopher read a paper in support of a version of determinism. (That should of course be redrafted into a determinist "language" about the production of various sounds and various pages being turned over, but let us take this description as a shorthand for that one.) Interested in this paper, I wrote asking for a copy of it. His letter in reply urged that no finished text of the paper existed since "his causal antecedents had been unfavourable": this, of course, amounts to a determinist way of saying that he had not got around to working on the paper, or typing it up, or some such. There was no obvious way for such a determinist to respond consistently to this request: free will defenders would characterize the occurrence in terms his actions (or inactions) here.

Conclusion

This chapter has presented in a clear fashion a determinist argument with the conclusion that the language of action is based on spurious contrasts and therefore the notion of action has no application: in effect, then, there are no actions, but only things that happen. If true, this conclusion should lead us to drop notions of (moral) responsibility. Notions of praise and blame are empty, since they imply (the possibility of) choice. (See also Chapter 5, p. 75) Rather, humans should be thought of like robots, with behaviour simply the working out of causal laws, just like the "behaviour" of clouds. In addition, I have urged the power of this argument: we cannot with good grace simply ignore its conclusions.

Faced with this argument, as with any, we might, first and most obviously, simply adopt the conclusions, or whatever the determinist equivalent of that would be. Putting that possibility aside, one might dispute the truth of some or all of the premises. Such possibilities will be considered in Chapters 4, 5 and 6. The third general way in which arguments might be contested is by suggesting some flaw in their logic: that the truth of the premises does not after all guarantee the truth of the conclusion. This idea will be considered in the next chapter, where discussion turns on the force of the determinist argument.

Determinism: qualifications and clarifications

Introduction

Initially, this chapter considers two lines of objection to the determinist argument, both rooted in the idea that it is not satisfactory as an argument. As noted previously, there are, in effect, three responses that might legitimately be made to any argument: the first is to accept its conclusion – to find it compelling. This means accepting both that the premises from which it is constructed are true and that the truth of the conclusion follows from the truth of the premises. (This idea of "following from" is what it means to speak of the argument as *valid*.) In passing, we see here one virtue of formalizing the determinist argument as we did (Chapter 2, p. 21): it allows us to identify and scrutinize the constituent premises.

However, someone planning to reject the conclusion of an argument must either (as a second response) reject one or more of the premises of that argument, reject the truth of the premises, as we might say; or (third response) must urge that the conclusion does not follow from those premises, reject the logic of the argument. In Chapter 2, some reasons to accept the truth of the premises were offered. The possibility of denying those premises will occupy us in Chapters 4, 5, 6, and 8. Here, though, I consider objections to the logic of the argument. These are, effectively, of three main types: objections to this argument, to the use of argument in this context, and to the supposed conclusion having the implications claimed by an argument such as this. I shall consider them in succeeding sections. I shall go on to consider some "objections" that, because they are pretty general, offer ways of elucidating further our account of determinism.

"This is no argument for determinism"

It might seem (despite the confidence of O'Connor 1971: p. 12) that the determinist argument is not *valid*: that the truth of its premises do not guarantee the truth of its conclusion. For, it might be thought, there are "gaps". In particular, the account of causal necessity does not follow simply from granting causation. Further, the incompatibility of causal necessity and choice is not explicitly asserted. Obviously, assessing the plausibility of the determinist argument is crucial here. As students of philosophy, we should reject arguments that are not well formed, and instead require their reformulation.

Faced with such objections, one strategy would indeed be to attempt to redraft or reformulate the argument to meet these objections. However, two considerations weigh heavily with me for leaving the argument as it is, and putting aside this line of objection. Initially, the direction of the argument is clear: to formulate every premise exactly (and to fill in any "gaps") will produce a longer and more complex argument, but will its force be any clearer? I think not, for (as acknowledged in Chapter 2) the key premises are the first, the second and the idea of causal necessity imported by the fourth. So, for a reader "ready to meet [the writer] . . . halfway – who does not begrudge a pinch of salt" (Frege 1960: 54), the formulation given above should prove satisfactory; certainly, it cannot simply be dismissed.

Further, three principles articulated in Chapter 2 support going along with the thrust of this argument, once the "pinch of salt" has been granted: first, the need to accommodate both the projects and the (apparent?) achievements of the natural sciences; second, the need to see ourselves as part of the natural world and (associatedly) to recognize our physical construction – this means, in part, a rejection of the "dualism" stated earlier; and third, the (apparent?) tension between the sorts of explanations given of actions and those given of, say, the kleptomaniac [KEY CASE 2], or in mitigation more generally. For it does seem that causes necessitate; that, as Flew puts it, "causes . . . do bring about their effects" (Flew & Vesey 1987:

174). Thus, if an effect is explained causally, "one couldn't do other-wise" than one did: this might be thought to apply to actions too. And this seems to explain everyday examples of mitigation, and the like; for example, where we conclude that Smith was not wholly responsible for the death of Jones, given his heart attack [KEY CASE 5] or given his brain tumour [KEY CASE 6]. So there does seem a lot to be said for the determinist's starting place.

In effect, then, the determinist asks us to reflect on the notions of choice and agency by pointing to cases in which free will defend-ers will prefer to treat human behaviour causally: since there are such cases (for example KEY CASE 2), a relevant difference must be identified between those cases and the occasions when some human behaviour (for example, our own) is to be treated in terms of agency. Such a plea for *consistency* (or accusation of inconsist-ency) is a primary tool in philosophy.

So (for all we have seen so far) the determinist argument should be allowed to stand: it embraces compelling principles, setting out a major problem for our consideration. To dismiss the argument as not yet fully formulated is foolhardy: it simply invites a longer, more complex version: better to have an argument with clearer contours, since we are sure it addresses our problem.

"Determinists cannot engage in arguments"

A more important objection builds on an oddity of determinism (Chapter 2, p. 33): that determinists' notions are incompatible with the whole idea of argument, so there cannot be an *argument* for determinism. For *reason*, *argument* and the like are not causal notions; so they are not open to the determinist. In this vein, I reported (Chapter 2, p. 34) a determinist "explaining" his not having done something by saying, "My causal antecedents were unfavourable", in a situation where free will defenders might have said, "I did not get round to doing it". Even claiming to *know* this appears to import non-causal notions, contrary to determinist assumptions. As Honderich (1993: 77) illustrates, this objection can be put in slightly different ways: as the claim that determinists are not entitled to such non-causal terms as "argument"; or as the claim that the truth of determinism makes all my supposed knowledge just another (causal) state of my body, more specifically of my brain.

Nevertheless, this objection can be met. First, the determinist simply employs his or her opponent's assumptions here. Beginning from an opponent's position, to show that this position involves inconsistencies, is a standard practice in philosophy: if successful, it can show one's opponent the inadequacy of his or her own position by his or her own lights.

In this case, the determinist offers a dilemma[1] to the free will defender: one horn of the dilemma involves acceptance of determinist accounts of human behaviour (accepting "the truth of determinism"). From this acceptance it would indeed flow that argument too was an illusion, since it imports non-causal notions such as *rational persuasion*. No free will defender could accept that!

The other horn comes from granting, "for the sake of argument", the free will defender's conception of rational process and argumentation: and then presenting him or her with an argument (roughly the one given above) for determinism (for "the truth of determinism")! In effect, this says, "If there are arguments (as you free will defenders say), here is an argument for determinism". So, by entertaining their opponents' assumptions, the determinists can undermine the position of those opponents.

This is a perfectly acceptable procedure: the determinist is not asserting the viability of argument in his or her own voice. He or she is a determinist, and therefore "adopts" the first horn of the dilemma (in so far as that does not involve a commitment to agency!). Hence the determinist can "argue", to this degree.

Of course, if determinism is correct, the free will defender will still go on "believing" that it is not. That is just a consequence of his or her brain and central nervous system being in a certain state. In this sense, there is no possibility of *believing* the opposite. And this person will indeed go on "acting" and "speaking" as though determinism were not true, where the scare-quotes indicate that this is not really action, since the notion of choice (fundamental to such a claim) is empty. One might indeed conclude (as above) that, if determinism is correct, that fact cannot possibly have a bearing on human behaviour; such behaviour is causally determined, including "opposition" to determinism.

Yet this suggests a second consideration, for if determinism is not correct, all accounts of human beings that (implicitly?) take it to be correct – for example, those employing computer modelling of human processes – will require modification. So the falsity of determinism is not trivial. But if its falsity is not trivial, its truth (or correctness) will not be either.

Thirdly, this is a substantive issue, not just one about words. As we saw in Chapter 1, the issue of mitigations (for example, asking, "Was this murder, in respect of the death of Jones [KEY CASES 4–6]?") is a genuine one. This is another way in which this discussion helps us get a clearer view of philosophy: it is not just about words for, here, the debate about what to *call* the event is also a debate about what to *do* with the (unfortunate?) driver, Smith. So that, even if the point is expressed as one about what *word* to use, it is in no sense a dispute in semantics. The choice between the words "murder" and "manslaughter" is a substantive choice!

In this way, the determinist's argument requires the free will defender to fulfil an obligation that he or she should already acknowledge: the obligation to sort out where causality does apply to human behaviour, since human behaviour can sometimes be viewed causally. Of course, the determinist adds the rider that this task cannot be fulfilled: that all human behaviour is causally explicable. But exactly that possibility should be considered by any robust free will defence. For this reason, it is appropriate to see the determinist argument as something a free will defender must formulate. So that, even if we acknowledged that determinists themselves cannot consistently engage in arguments, there will still be a determinist argument (constructed by free will defenders) to be met.

In conclusion, then, there seems no compelling reason why we should think of the logic of the argument as either flawed in detail (p. 36) or precluded on principle (p. 37). Is there another line of objection?

"Actions are caused, but by motives etc."

Another such line begins from the thought that determinism has no frightening implications, because actions viewed as actions are caused too, although they are caused by motives, intentions and the like. So that we should think of motives, etc. as operating causally; but without the "could not do otherwise". Rather, causation by motives and the like might be the sort of thing a free will defender could embrace. Thus it might seem that the causality did not after all preclude choice, in some sense. This position might be reinforced by introducing a distinction between "agent causation" and "event causation" (Flew & Vesey 1987: 9), with the first being that kind of causation centrally involving humans as "originators" or "initiators". Causal necessity for *agent causation* might then be thought not to preclude choice, even if other kinds of causation (event causation) did.

Before beginning, notice that the project in this section is a relatively modest one: the objection is that there is something amiss in the logic of the determinist argument; that the premises do not compel the conclusion. So the strategy is to meet that objection *only*, by showing how this position readily turns itself into a denial of one or more of the premises of the argument, rather than an objection to its logic. Of course, this simply puts aside questions of the adequacy of the argument until we consider its premises (in Chapters 4, 5, 6 and 8).

But agent causation, then, must be *causation* in (at least) the sense (a) of being part of a causal chain – that is, not self-initiated – and (b) of involving causal necessity. The first constraint follows from the thought that every event has a cause (determinist premise 1): for the event that is the piece of agent causation must itself have a cause, and hence be part of a causal chain.[2] (Lest this seem too strong a constraint, let it be granted that this principle only goes back as far as the beginning of time: say, to the Big Bang, or to the Genesis-type creation, or whenever.)

Yet how is the determinist conclusion to be resisted on any account of causation obedient to these constraints? For the necessitation of a particular event (in (b)) from the prior link in the causal chain (in (a)) will make that event inevitable (given the antecedent state of the world): so there is no room for choice: the agent causation (according to this view) would be as inexorable as any other. Of course, there might still be a reason (for instance, parsimoniousness in theory-construction) for denying the possibility of a distinctive *agent causation*, but this contrast between agent causation and some other kind cannot be used to reject the conclusion of the determinist argument.

That it might seem to do so derives from twin dangers implicit in countenancing *agent causation*: that its defenders tend to deny (in theory or in practice) either (a) or (b) above. So that (denying (a)) they think of agent causation as self-initiated. But, as we have noticed, in such a case the events that constitute the agent causation will not themselves be the effects of earlier causes: hence they will be uncaused (contrary to premise 1 of the determinist argument). So, meeting this form of objection involves considering the plausibility of that premise (see Chapter 4).

Equally, ([denying (b)) they think of the agent causation as not causally necessitated: yet that seems to admit the possibility of "same *cause*, different *effect*", which seems contrary to conceiving of the matter as a causal one. Indeed, it seems contrary to a characterization as causal to admit that the very same cause might generate a different effect: that, say, the very same position of balls on a billiards table might result in a different outcome, with nothing else being different [KEY CASE 8]. So, again, this will involve the denial of one premise of the determinist argument (probably premise 2), a topic for Chapters 5, 6 and 8. And, of course, combining these two denials simply combines the two problems.

For these reasons, then, distinguishing agent causation from another kind does not look like a plausible strategy here.

Is the conclusion important?

Another difficulty involves questioning whether the conclusion of the determinist argument is *important*. In effect, our response is already in place, for, as we saw above (p. 39), the free will defender too will need to consider such a position, since it can result from consistent application (that is, application to all human behaviour) of ideas he or she already applies to some behaviour (for example, mitigations).

As Berlin asks (if determinism were true): "what reasons can you, in principle, adduce for attributing responsibility or applying moral rules to [people] which you would not think it reasonable to apply in the case of compulsive choosers – kleptomaniacs, dipsomaniacs, and the like?" (quoted in Watson 1982: 97)". Since we agree that Berlin's "compulsive choosers" are not agents, not morally responsible, this question can turn back upon itself: we did not attribute responsibility to them, so why should we ever do so? I am not (yet) suggesting that an answer cannot be found. But one is owed.

Moreover, this way of putting the problem shows its connection to other concerns, since even we free will defenders regularly see the behaviour of the kleptomaniac [KEY CASE 2] or the dipsomaniac (Berlin's example) as resulting from "circumstances beyond the agent's control". So this way of conceptualizing behaviour is something we (partially) share with the determinist.

Yet if all my behaviour, including my thought, is (causally) determined, my thinking that I have (or have not) a refutation of determinism is likewise determined; hence it cannot constitute a *genuine* refutation (see p. 37). Or, from the other side, since (given the "truth" of determinism) it is inevitable that I will think *X* or *Y* – say, assent to determinism – that thought is not changeable by reason, but only by other causal forces. Hence, if I presently "accept" an argument for determinism, that fact is as causally determined as any other. In this way, the "truth" (or otherwise) of determinism cannot possibly make a difference: if my causal antecedents are such that my brain is in such-and-such a state, then I assert determinism; if they are different, my brain is (perhaps) in a different state and now I assert some free will defence. But these events are as determined as any other.

The bleakness of this picture is one key feature here. Suppose we were to find that the "arguments" for it could not be refuted; this would not make the matter any worse. Nevertheless, we find it depressing just because this is not how we view ourselves (as was noted in Chapter 1, p. 4).

The plausibility of the alternative

Supposing that one wishes to counter the threat posed by the determinist argument. What should one do? A simplified version of arguments from van Inwagen (1983) can be considered here, in two parts.

The first element argues for the incompatibility of free will and causation, by urging that, if universal causation is true, then laws of nature (together with an account of the state of the universe leading up to my birth) ensure just what physical (and psychological) "movements" I will make. Hence there can be no choosing: and that is our determinist conclusion. As van Inwagen (1983: 53) concludes, I could refrain from making those movements only if I could have changed either the laws of nature or the initial conditions. But clearly both suggestions are plain crazy. So (van Inwagen urges) universal causation and free will are incompatible. And universal causation is the first premise of our determinist argument.

Now, van Inwagen thereby accepts the logic of the determinist argument: that is, he accepts that *if* there is universal causation, it follows that the notion of choice cannot apply. So, for him, granting that universal causation is incompatible with free will is recognizing that determinism is incompatible with free will. (For us, the second of these is self-evident: the determinist argument concludes that free will is illusory. But the first remains contentious: van Inwagen's version of incompatibilism, unlike ours, urges the incompatibility of universal causality and choice.)

Second, van Inwagen asserts: "If incompatibilism is true, then either determinism or the free-will thesis is false. To deny the free-will thesis would be to deny the existence of moral responsibility, which would be absurd . . . Therefore, we should reject determinism" (1983: 223). Consider the form of this argument: in effect, it says, "Either A or B (and not both): but denying B means denying C, which is absurd. Therefore deny A". Structurally, this argument asks us to accept free will because the alternative would be giving up moral responsibility. (There is a complication here, in a part of the passage not quoted, to which I will return.) But this cannot be an argument against the determinist since, for him or her, giving up moral responsibility is precisely one hoped-for outcome. So this line of argument simple assumes as false what our determinist takes to be true. Before returning to this point, it is worth introducing two complications. For, as we shall see, van Inwagen's argument is not quite this one.

Notice that we can also get another result out of the argument-form described above by simply asserting the *truth* of determinism: then it would read (roughly), "Either A or B (and not both); and A – therefore not-B (whatever the consequences)". But van Inwagen aims to block this line of argument: so the centre of the passage omitted from the quotation above reads: "Moreover there seems to be no good reason to accept determinism" (van Inwagen 1983: 223). But that cannot be our position, at least: for presently we do have before us a good reason to accept determinism, based on the determinist argument. So, while van Inwagen seeks to block this loop-hole, we are not (yet?) in a position to do so.

Our position, then, is not that reached by attentive readers at the end of van Inwagen's book: but our position is clarified, first, by noting how, for van Inwagen, the issue is really between (universal) causality and freedom. Of course, if this contrast can be maintained, the only kind of free will defence will be one that denies universal causality. But has van Inwagen given us reason to take that line? Second, we look at a principle adopted by van Inwagen, namely, that: "if anyone *can* (i.e. has it within his powers to) render some proposition false, then that proposition is not a law of physics" (1983: 54). The difficulties cluster around the term "can".

One problem here is the sense in which something *can* happen. Suppose some law of nature predicts that some planet will be in some quadrant in the night sky at some time. Suppose further that this really is a law of nature, describing this planet's motion exactly. Now, all (accurate) observations of this planet will indeed conform to the predictions: so could such a "theory' be found false (falsified) even in principle? That is to say, could the planet appear elsewhere (in principle)? Imagining the following scenario, we might say, "yes": I predict the planet will be in a quadrant different to that implied by the theory – if the planet were to show up there, the theory would be falsified. Since the empirical nature of natural science guarantees that this just might happen (although it is deeply improbable), the theory would be falsifiable in principle (Chalmers 1999: 62–3). Such a conception of falsifiability proves too much: for any claim can be falsified in this sense. So we should withhold assent to van Inwagen's principle, for what can be proved false (in principle) might none the less be a law of physics!

The difficulty is to see what "John can render this proposition false" means, beyond such a case. For any proposition describing a state of the world will be falsifiable in principle: the point is just that it cannot actually be falsified. So, when van Inwagen asks if "John could render some proposition false" (1983: 55), we must see that there is a sense here of needing to render it false *within the laws of nature*: hence, that this procedure is not a helpful one.

So we have seen that we (as yet) have no good reason to reject determinism, faced with the determinist argument. Hence we cannot make the choice van Inwagen (1983: 223) suggests. For us, recognizing conflict between determinism and responsibility – granting the incompatibility of free will (and responsibility) with determinism – gives no reason to choose one way rather than another; or (perhaps) a reason to "choose" determinism, as at least we have an argument in that direction.

This leads us back to an earlier point: that views such as van Inwagen's simply assume as false what our determinist takes to be true. At the least, there seems to be no general objection to determinist argumentation here. To succeed, such a line of argument must somehow use the *fact* that there is a tension between responsibility and determinism as a reason to deny one of the premises of the determinist argument. As we shall see (Chapter 5), the "utilitarian" position offers just such a view. (But such a line also considers the (possible) compatibility of free will and causality (see also Chapter 6).)

Two further issues (which have loomed large in discussions of free will in recent philosophy) might have been included here, since they concern the nature of determinism. Both suggest that the contrasts between responsibility and non-culpability and between free will and determinism do not line up as smoothly as has been suggested here (although, recall, the determinist argument (Chapter 2, p. 21) is against the possibility of (genuine) choice, rather than against morality as such). These are, first, a view of determinism as "irrelevant" (P. Strawson 1974: 19: and see Chapter 7, p. 100), that "we never in fact cease to see others as responsible beings simply as a result of accepting deterministic explanations" (Watson 1982: 5); second, the possibility (canvassed by Frankfurt 1969: see van Inwagen 1983: 162–82; Fischer 1994: 131–51) that moral responsibility might be combined with a kind of determinism, where an agent is responsible despite no alternative action being open to him or her (Chapter 7, p. 105).

However, given the technicality of these views, and their relation to psychological determinism, and further, given that they are seen most clearly in the light of later issues, discussion of them has been postponed until Chapter 7. As we shall see, there is reason to think that they do not meet the determinist's challenge.

Is there a possibility of psychological determinism?

Earlier, it was urged that the causes the determinist refers to should be taken as *physical* causes; and hence the position adopted was a physical determinism, where this meant, roughly,[3] those causes employed in contemporary physics. And that position was defended as being the most powerful version of determinism because it arrived at determinist conclusions from the (universal) causation of science (alone?). It should be contrasted with accounts of determinism that understand the notion of causation at a human level; as the result of human psychology or economic activity, or the progress of history, or such like. In fact, I shall concentrate on the psychological since these other versions are to some degree or other equivalent to it. In doing so, I am temporarily putting aside the commitment made in Chapter 2 to discuss determinism where the notion of *causation* is explained via the procedures of "hard sciences" (for example, physics). Our strategic interest here lies in the way in which the determinist argument operates through the notion of causal necessity. For how plausible are psychological constraints as similarly necessitating? This is to question the plausibility of psychological (etc.) laws.[4]

Notice how other forms of determinism (for instance, economic determinism) can amount to psychological determinism. As Kenny (1992a: 143) puts it, "[a]ny determinism in virtue of economic laws will . . . be psychological determinism", since:

> it uses mentalistic notions in the identification of its data and the formulation of its laws. Passing a dollar bill voluntarily over the counter is an economic phenomenon in the sense in which accidentally dropping a dollar bill down a drain is not: this is a distinction which can only be systematically applied in virtue of the relevant notion of *voluntariness*, which is a psychological concept.   (Kenny 1992a: 143)

Even when we think of, say, the workers' choices as heavily constrained ("determined") by their class position or the power of monopoly capitalism of a certain sort, we still regard individual workers as choosing – although their choices may be the result of advertising, of the pressures of the labour market, and so on. So confronting psychological determinism is also confronting other attempts to derive deterministic conclusions from general remarks about collections of (free) agents. Kenny usefully summarizes the general position; that: "someone with a complete knowledge of the histories of individuals and societies, and a complete mastery of the laws of the appropriate disciplines, would in principle be able to forecast the future" (1992a: 142). But how plausible a thesis is that, in either its specifically psychological or more general form?

I shall urge that the closer we get to a "causal law", the further we get from that law's referring to the agent's psychology, while, if we make clear and unambiguous reference to that psychology, we do not approach plausible causal laws, especially if we think of such laws as exceptionless.

Three ground rules are central here. First, human beings must be recognized as physical systems; hence the psychological should be seen as *dependent* in some way or other on the physical. Although disputable, this point preserves causal continuities in ways that the project of science would tend to support. As Putnam remarks: "Very few people any longer suppose that living beings violate any laws of physics, or that human beings have immaterial souls which cause them to move in ways that violate laws governing the conservation of momentum" (1992: 83). Certainly, it is part of the project of twentieth-century science (here, neuroscience) that there are no such "gaps" in causality: persons are "complex material systems" (Nagel 1979: 181).

Second, arbitrariness must be avoided: that is, human behaviour is explicable. Free will defenders would certainly want actions performed to be *explicable* – for example, in terms of reasons, motives, intentions or such like – rather than for their occurrence to be mysterious. And one might well think (see Chapter 4, p. 55) that causality was required if such explicability is to be maintained.

Third, some views might be mistaken for psychological determinism. For example, Dennett considers the case of someone who is likely to rape. Fearing that I will be "overcome by lust" and rape a young woman I find walking alone:

> I educate myself about the horrors of rape from the woman's point of view, and enliven my sense of the brutality of the crime so that if I happen to meet [a voluptuous woman walking

> unescorted in a deserted place] . . . I am *unable* to do the awful
> things I would have done otherwise.
>
> (Dennett 1984: 134, original emphasis)

As Dennett recognizes, such educating of oneself requires that one
be an agent here: someone *decides* to do something, and brings it
about. No doubt the method used here might have been causal: not
education, but "aversion therapy", or shock-treatment. But the
decision was freely taken (compare KEY CASE 3). This cannot be our
model for the psychologically determined, for behaviour thus
amenable to education is certainly not (causally) determined in the
determinist's sense.

Clearly, the determinist can appeal to the impact of experiences
on the distinctive psychologies of particular individuals. But, for
determinism, the sorts of interactions envisaged must be strictly
causal; that (say) genuine *learning*, of the kind that presupposes
agency, is not included. This is the problem of really being a determinist when one grants a sufficiently rich psychology to humankind. A second difficulty runs in the opposite direction. What are
we to make, say, of remarks concerning changing brain-states: for
example, neurones firing? For factors such as these look like the
causal story "behind" the psychology. But they represent biophysi-
cal mechanisms, rather than psychological ones. Hence, although
they offer a route to a determinism, it is not to psychological
determinism. Of course, these considerations cannot refute
psychological determinism, nor are they intended to do so.

A common-sense objection to psychological determinism notes
that reasons do not function as causes (Kenny 1992a: 144–5). We
can do X for a reason, or even without a reason, whereas, if the first
premise of the determinist argument is accepted, a causal story can
always be told. Philosophers have rightly emphasized the different
operation (the different "logic") of the terms "reason" and "cause"
(see Chapter 6, p. 82). As White notes: "A person's reason for doing
X must contain reference either to X or to something which is
thought by the agent to be a means to X" (1968: 17). But this does
not apply to causes: for instance, huge numbers of causal interactions (in my brain, musculature, etc.) are involved in my typing these
words: I do not know those interactions, but they are genuinely (part
of) the causal "story" for this event. Similarly, putative causes are

either effect-producing or they are not, whereas reasons "can be good or bad, defensible or indefensible" (White 1968: 17).

If reasons do not operate causally, that might give us a basis for refuting a determinism couched exclusively in terms of human psychology, especially if such psychology were primarily a description of reasons for action. For that account of causality seems ultimately to deliver determinist conclusions. It is even more tempting to think that determinism's refutation *requires* such a move, but this is mistaken. Even some who think reasons *operate* causally (for example Davidson 1980: xii) do not accept that psycho-physical laws can be formulated; without them, the relevant notion of a cause has no purchase here.

Notice, too, that thus differentiating causation allows the possibility of refuting psychological determinism with arguments that leave physical determinism unscathed.[5]

"Determined by one's personality"?

A revealing objection here might be that all my behaviour is determined by my personality, and by the history that has caused me to have the personality I do (to be the person that I am). So I am bound to, say, help the aged person in distress when I meet that person in the street. This is a consequence of my being who I am, itself a consequence of my history. In this sense, I "could not do otherwise" than I do. A determinism of this sort, it might be argued, is both appealing and unthreatening (see p. 39). Further, my acting "out of character" (say, by not helping that aged person) is also explicable: something in my (recent?) history explains it too.

Is this a "non-threatening" determinism? Certainly, the factors it mentions, in my history and education, are ones a free will defender could endorse. Much here turns on whether the term "determined" identifies the sort of causal determination (importing causal necessity) discussed by the determinist. If not, nothing in this case need worry us: its advocate is not a determinist at all! Read as advocating determinism, this position has indeed all the threatening characteristics identified in Chapter 2: people are not agents, the notion of choice does not apply to them. In making out this example, its advocate must show not merely that my behaviour "flows" from who I am (which might well be granted by free will defenders, especially those who recognize that we learn to make choices)[6] but that this behaviour *causally* results from my experiences. My previous life must be thought of entirely causally. This would preclude the notion of *learning* being applied to me. "Learning" is an essentially non-causal notion (at least once stimulus-response behaviour is contrasted with genuine learning: see Toulmin 1969: 89–94). Finding any behavioural outcomes not causally explicable would refute this view, by providing a counter-example to its claims. If there were once a person somewhere whose behaviour were not causally explicable in this way, the view under consideration would be false. Can this be ruled out prior to investigation? What, except a prior commitment to determinism, requires that the outcomes *must* be causal? For even when the event is simply, say, my walking across the room [KEY CASE 1], persons can act "out of character" and do things "for no reason" (that is, where no explanation is forthcoming, and perhaps none needed). Of course, one might, say, appeal to our general principle (determinism premise 1: Chapter 2, p. 21) that every event has a cause. Now the behaviour must be causally explicable just because all events are so explicable. Yet now nothing in the explanation refers to what is distinctively human: the appeal is no longer to determinism of the human psyche or psychology, but to a general causal determinism. And that case is best (and most powerfully) made out by recognizing causality at a level shared with the rest of the universe, rather than one (the human level) not shared in this way. Thus psychological determinism cannot be the option for us to consider.

Does this conclusion follow from the distinctiveness of humans? Can one expect causal laws for psychology that apply to more than single individuals, since we are all unique? Two responses (other than simply denying that humans differ that radically) are, first, to grant our uniqueness but insist that our constituent parts (particles and the like) are not unique. There can be laws, etc. that apply to them; and hence that determine the behaviour of the material of which our bodies are constituted. But these are laws from natural science, so this not *psychological* determinism. The second option grants that each of us has a unique psychology. Were this true, it would provide a reason to be doubtful about the prospect of causal laws of human psychology, and hence of the prospects of a psychological determinism. With either option, the most plausible version of determinism is indeed the one employing physical causation.

Conclusion

This chapter results in a revitalized determinist argument: at first blush (at least), the deterministic conclusions urged earlier should be taken seriously, for we have found neither a substantial general argument against determinism, nor any refutation of determinism in detailed criticisms of its general argument. Of course, other arguments might be adduced (although those considered here reflect some typical arguments).

It must be acknowledged that, having failed to refute an argument, one need not automatically accept its conclusions, although, in the absence of any counter-arguments, failing to do so will be odd. (In the same vein, having refuted the given argument for a certain position does not prove that position wrong: rather, it simply leaves one with no reason (yet) to accept it.)

Still, given that one has an (articulated) argument for determinist conclusions and, as yet, no substantial reasons to reject them, we should go into later chapters disposed to be determinists if we cannot rebut determinist contentions.

Moreover, we have clarified the nature of any determinist conclusions, giving reasons why (for determinists) the causality at work will be physical, since confronting *psychological determinism* (that is, determinism that claims that the causal story for actions operates at the level of the psychology of the "agent") is not confronting the strongest form of determinism: psychological "laws" are less plausibly understood in terms of causal necessity (determinist premise 4) than are physical laws. Or, to put that another way, there are no genuine laws in psychological understanding of action. But this fact can escape notice since, sometimes, exception-bearing generalizations function quite satisfactorily in psychological explanations and, at other times, an implicit physical explanation (say, in genetics) is appealed to.

4 Libertarianism: two varieties

Introduction

As noted towards the end of Chapter 2 and again in Chapter 3, the conclusion of any argument can be contested either by disputing the truth of some or all of the argument's premises or by denying that the conclusion follows from those premises. In that vein, this chapter will consider opposition to determinism based on denying the truth of the first premise of our determinist argument (Chapter 2, p. 21): that every event has a cause. (Later chapters will consider other premises.) Traditionally, those who deny the truth of the premise that every event has a cause are called "libertarians": although this name may not be completely happy, I will use it here to pick up that philosophical tradition.

Does libertarianism provide a satisfactory answer to the challenge of the determinist argument? If not, does it nevertheless shed light on what free will defenders must acknowledge? And a *satisfactory* answer is of course one that has an "exact fit" with our examples of unfreedom or constraint (such as KEY CASES 2 & 6) and with our examples of free action, such as walking across the room [KEY CASE 1], drinking a glass of water, and so on: actions that will be free if any are.

Two ways of denying that every event has a cause identify two versions of libertarianism. First, one might urge that *some* events were uncaused so it was not true that every event has a cause, an option to be considered in the next section. Alternatively, one might argue that *no* events have causes, so it is not true that any event had a cause, a position exemplified below (p. 60).

The Campbell position

The first variant of libertarianism for consideration, then, urges that there are *some* uncaused events: that, while for some events a causal chain (a chain of causal connections) can be drawn that leads invariably to them, another class of events involves breaks in such causal chains. Libertarians differ, of course, as to what events are uncaused in this sense, and how such uncaused events come about. As a specific example, consider the views of Campbell.[1] Since our interest in this text lies partly in learning about argument, it is useful to go slowly, making each stage of our discussion fully explicit. This involves giving exposition of key elements of Campbell's account, and then looking at replies to it. In this way, consideration of this case can show us how to articulate a putative counter-case, and a counter-blast to one.

Campbell's position was chosen both because it provides a clear example of a position of this kind,where some (but not all) human behaviour is *not* caused, and because it exemplifies the difficulties of such a position. That it is rather old and unfashionable should not divert us from these virtues.

Campbell's position is typical of an argumentative strategy used by libertarians. He urges that there are discontinuities in causal chains in respect of moral decisions. From his writings it is not clear whether moral decisions are just one example of such causal discontinuity, although his arguments suggest that perhaps they are the only case where such discontinuities occur.[2] Campbell argues that human decisions and actions can arise, on the one hand, from *inclination* (following what one wants to do[3]) or, on the other, from *duty*. If they are done from inclination then, according to Campbell, causal continuity is preserved.[4] If, however, they are done from duty then, Campbell urges, causal continuity is not preserved. And, Campbell suggests, introspection makes it quite clear to us that, when acting against our strongest desires or wants, we are combating causal forces. All this can be located in our familiar experience, through introspection. To think otherwise, Campbell says, is to take a paralytic's-eye view of action.[5]

Of course, Campbell would grant that, in one sense, my behaviour in those cases where I do my duty is determined, but by my duty (by where my duty lies). And this is not a determinist kind of "determined"; it does not amount to the working out of a chain of causes. Rather, it comes about just because I do not act in accordance with my inclinations. That another person (one of less character) might not have done his or her duty illustrates that the events here are not determined. What occurs follows from my "acts of will": and those (for Campbell) are counter-causal.

Campbell's argument does explain (or seem to) why free will is appropriately ascribed to human beings but not, for example, to tables: that humans can have duties. Relatedly, it trades heavily on the distinction between actions done from duty and actions done from inclination.[6] For (according to Campbell) only actions done from duty operate counter-causally. And, since it is hard to think of a duty that does not impose a moral obligation, it seems right to take moral actions as the only ones that are uncaused. Further, this argument places great weight on evidence from introspection. In this way, it is typical of our pre-reflective views for the freedom of our actions – describable in quasi-libertarian ways: that (rather than feeling causally determined) we *feel* ourselves to be agents, making choices; and recognize this in our own behaviour. So Campbell's position shares a great deal with common-sense.

Criticisms of Campbell

A determinist's powerful objections to Campbell's position show both something about determinism and something about Campbell. The first objection turns on Campbell's evidence; on his use of introspection. For the determinist has already urged that introspection, establishing at best that one *feels* free (Ginet 1990: 91), is beside the point here. A kleptomaniac [KEY CASE 2] may think he or she is acting freely and still not be free, so introspective evidence cannot be decisive in the way Campbell urges. Thus the kleptomaniac might think that he or she had free choice when he or she took the scarf from the department store, and might assure us (when we ask) that he or she did. Similarly, a person with a certain sort of brain tumour might be convinced that he or she was freely doing something. One can even imagine a drug that not only compelled certain behaviour, but that also gave those taking it the feeling that they were freely choosing to do that thing. In all these cases, constrained behaviour occurred, despite the participant feeling free. So, far from being a paralytic's-eye view of action to ignore the evidence of introspection, it is (the determinist says) the plainest of common-sense. For what must be explained is what the person *does*, and not what that person thinks or feels he or she has done. That is a matter of considering the physical movements (and omissions), not appealing to "acts of will". This simply repeats the recognition, noted in the exposition of determinism (Chapter 2, p. 30), that one's feeling of freedom was beside the point.

As a second objection, the determinist attacks Campbell's distinction between actions done from *duty* and those done from *inclination*. That contrast is nothing like as firm as Campbell suggests: choices are not *obviously* either from desire *or* moral. For example, one might regard a philanthropist as regularly doing things it was the duty of humankind to do (say, looking after other humans) but that the philanthropist did because he or she was so inclined: that was what made him or her a philanthropist! Here, duty and inclination coincide. To convince us of the centrality of the contrast between duty and inclination, Campbell emphasizes the possibility of a conflict between them: for example, my duty to look after my sick mother conflicts with, say, my inclination to go to the beach to get a suntan. Recall that Campbell's argument for any action being counter-causal is based on such conflict. But there can be conflicts within one's inclinations, desires or wants: and also conflicts within one's duties. For instance, I would very much like another drink because it would make me feel good now, but I would also like very much to have a clear head tomorrow morning, and another drink will ensure tomorrow's hangover. Here, two in-clinations conflict. In resolving them, one doesn't think of conflicting causes in such a case, as one might on Campbell's line. Again, my duty to my country might lead me to inform on a spy but my duty to a friend might lead me not to inform on the spy, if the spy were my friend. If conflict *alone* were to suggest the over-coming of causal forces, as Campbell suggests, there would be a plethora of counter-causal cases (or, rather, of cases of conflicting causes).

Such points show, of course, that Campbell's argument here is extremely weak: the key distinction he employs is ill-founded.[7] When we add the conclusion drawn in the previous consideration, that his "evidence" does not prove his point, little is really left to lead us in the direction Campbell wants.

Of course, Campbell's conclusion might still be true, even though the argument given for it is weak or unsatisfactory. So we must continue to look for a real refutation of Campbell's position. (But, having no argument for Campbell's position, and the determinist's argument for a contrary position, the balance of probabilities must presently be against Campbell.)

The two sorts of problem for Campbell's position just noted can be reinforced by citing a third. Suppose that Campbell takes moral decisions to be the only place where there are uncaused events: these are the only examples he gives, and the only basis for location of the counter-causal is an action done from duty and against inclination, such duties typically having a moral element. Then Campbell's position concedes that most of our actions follow inclination and hence preserve causal continuity. For those actions, the determinist is perfectly right, according to Campbell. Thus, the oddity of Campbell's view is that it cannot *save* enough. We turned to libertarianism to combat determinism not just in respect of actions done from duty but in respect of all our actions: examples of free action should include my walking across the room because I wanted to [KEY CASE 1]. According to Campbell's view, since these (presumably) follow my inclinations, they would not be free actions. So adopting Campbell's position cannot secure enough for the opponents of determinism. Even if conceded, this position could not establish that the determinist was not at least largely correct.

Taken together, these three oddities within Campbell's view make the position very unappealing, for it does not secure the range of free action hoped for, and is not well served by arguments. Still, none of these are genuine reasons for not adopting Campbell's position, although they may amount to either (a) reasons why one might not want to, or (b) an absence of reasons why one should adopt this view.

A major difficulty here, typical as a criticism of libertarianism, is that this view flies in the face of science. Applied to Campbell's position, this will involve a rejection of his argument, since, negatively, modern scientific studies do not detect causal discontinuities in respect of some actions rather than others. The same story of electrical and chemical activity in the brain applies in both cases. Further, positively, the kinds of "acts of will" to which Campbell appeals are not required by causal explanation; nor are they "locatable" within the pattern of causal explanation. So, as a matter of fact, Campbell's account conflicts with the *conclusions* of science. This alone represents an objection to it.

But, more importantly, Campbell's account conflicts with the *project* of science. After all, this is how the determinist supports the first premise of his own argument. The project of science surely involves the hunt for causal continuities, and nothing will escape this search. Consider, for example, some inexplicable phenomenon, such as the Bermuda Triangle (Chapter 2, p. 23). Grant that contemporary science has nothing to say on this topic. Yet surely our expectation is that, eventually, some explanation of the phenomenon in question will be found. And it will resemble other explanations given by scientists, highlighting some kinds of causal forces (although perhaps of kinds not presently recognized). Further, we are familiar with just this sort of case. For example, medicine accepts acupuncture by identifying drug-like secretions (endorphins) stimulated in acupuncture. That is, the seemingly mysterious is integrated into the scientific understanding. And that is the point about the *project* of science: we assume, with justification, that scientific investigation can be applied to everything. Since that investigation does imply the search for causal stories, Campbell has "got it wrong", not just about the detail but, as it were, as a matter of policy. Thus Campbell's argument is no good, as the required discontinuities do not exist, and, further, accepting Campbell's position requires us to give up the achievements of science, to no longer regard them as achievements. So Campbell's position is untenable.

Campbell's position can show us a final point: for, far from restoring (the possibility of) freedom, this kind of libertarianism (and perhaps any kind?) might seem to remove its main prop. As Hume notes:

> Now necessity [has] . . . been allow'd to belong to the will of man, and no one has ever pretended to deny, that we can draw inferences concerning human actions, and that those inferences are founded on the experienc'd union of like actions with like motives and circumstances.   (1978 [1740]: 457)

In permitting discontinuities in causal chains, in allowing actions to be unpredictable (the point of Campbell's moves[8]), the position allows actions to be random. That is to say, "uncaused" is there equated with "unpredictable" and (hence) with "random" (compare Ayer 1954: 275).

This is something of a "visceral" objection, rather than one that identifies a major difficulty for the libertarian. But it reinforces the idea that, once free will is granted, behaviour must still (typically) be explicable in principle: indeed, that it makes no sense to talk of *free action* if that "action" results from anything beyond the will of the agent, and hence anything beyond his or her control, as a random event would obviously be.

Arguments of the kind in this objection have been influential against libertarians, since free will defenders require (at least in some cases) reliable and explicable outcomes of actions, which can seem to require causal continuity. For my (freely) walking across the room [KEY CASE 1] must be that: my walking across the room for a reason, or for no reason. But in some sense the action flows from a choice of mine: my wanting to pick up the glass and my doing so are related here. There is a causal story to be told at least about my picking up the glass. Certainly, we might expect *truly* random actions to be inexplicable. Moreover, the idea of an action being random is used as a reason for not blaming someone. To say of a person that she acted out of character, for example, is to offer an excuse for some action or choice that seems random.

However, does "uncaused" equal "random"? If not, this line of objection cannot get going. Notice that, in the "out of character" example above, the person might be acting in accordance with some causal law, just an unusual (for that person) one. Moreover, a standard way of introducing "randomness" might be by throwing dice: yet the movement of dice is strictly causally determined. If this were our model for the random, again, there is no reason to associate the random with the uncaused.

Morals from consideration of Campbell

Consideration of Campbell's position has highlighted three key constraints on any satisfactory account of free will. First, it must do justice to the project of science, rather than fly in its face. So that Campbell-type causal discontinuities cannot be accommodated within a project for the causal explanation of phenomena. Second, and relatedly, there is no room here for appeals beyond the bounds of the laws of science; no room for "acts of will" unless their causal base is clearly explained. Third, the evidential basis for any account must be stronger than just introspection. Determinism is built around these fundamental insights: that a modern account of persons must be materialist in the (limited) sense that persons are comprised of matter, and that changes in the states of such matter are causally explicable.

As a fourth point, any satisfactory account must explain (as Campbell's seeks to) `how free will is the *special* province of humankind. So accounts of action must have an "exact fit" here: that what are taken to be actions turn out to be so on the account (KEY CASE 1, for instance), and that our cases of unfreedom or constraint turn out *not* to be actions on that account. Campbell gets this wrong. For him, only some of what we take as free actions would turn out to be free, because only they originate from duty rather than inclination. To repeat, my walking across the room just because I want to, a central case of a free action for most free will defenders, would not count as free for Campbell. But, also, only free actions should turn out to be free: an account that made our kleptomaniac [KEY CASE 2] a free agent would, for that reason, be wrong. Relatedly, the account must ascribe freedom to *agents*, such as persons, and not to the inanimate: it must explain why the province of agency is located where it is. As we saw, Campbell has an answer here: only those with duties could be agents on his account and, while that account is flawed, we can take this insight from it.

The idea of uncertainty (from physics) – two versions

The second variety of libertarianism considered takes its starting point from a thesis of contemporary physics, Heisenberg's uncertainty principle. As with Campbell's position, this view consists in the denial of premise 1 of the determinist argument: that is, it asserts that it is not true that every event has a cause. But according to this version, *no* events have causes, in the requisite sense. The position claims this result as the outcome of a thesis rooted in science, and hence, its defenders would say, cannot be flying in the face of science.[9]

The relevant consideration is Heisenberg's *uncertainty principle*. To explain this idea, begin by considering an ordinary, everyday particle, such as a football. For such an object, its position and its velocity "define" its relevant properties (we should have to add its size, too, but this can be ignored for the moment). Once we add the causal laws, we can predict its behaviour from these properties, together with those laws. So these are the characteristic particle properties. Now, some explanations in physics employ the idea of an *elementary* particle – one of the fundamental building blocks of matter. Then, if the position and velocity of such an elementary particle are precisely known, we should be able to "define" its relevant properties, and hence write causal laws in respect of it. Heisenberg's uncertainty principle states that this is impossible: that the more closely we can specify the position of an elementary particle, the less exactly we can know or describe its velocity, and vice versa. So, in practice, physicists might deal with a fairly close specification of each, and thus talk of a particle in roughly such-and-such a place, with roughly such-and-such velocity characteristics (to put the matter in everyday language), and this will be so for whatever elementary particle one selects. For convenience, I talk here about electrons, but these points could be redrafted for hadrons, leptons, quarks, or whatever is the state-of-the-art elementary particle for theoretical physics.

Since one can describe only the rough position of the electron and its rough velocity, causal laws describing the characteristics of such electrons can no longer be written. Or so the argument might run. This would identify clearly defined classes of uncaused events, namely, sub-atomic events. But since we are all composed of such particles (the argument might go), all or most bits of human behaviour *comprise* such uncaused events, at least at the most fundamental level of analysis.

Before turning to determinist responses to this position, two rather different ways of reading or interpreting the uncertainty principle should be noted, since the contrast between them will become important later on. The first interprets the uncertainty principle as a constraint on human knowledge: an elementary particle no doubt *has* a determinate position and velocity, but this cannot be known. For example, this limitation of human knowledge could be explained because the smallest "item" we could use to investigate or test the velocity of our electron would be a particle of light – a photon. And a photon is so very large, relative to our electron, as to disturb either its position or its velocity, or both. On this interpretation, the uncertainty operates, as it were, at the level of what it is possible for humans to know. (Call this the "knowledge-to-humans" interpretation.) On the second reading of the uncertainty principle, the constraint is one in nature. So that it makes *no sense* to ascribe to an elementary particle the properties regularly ascribed to ordinary, everyday particles like footballs, at least not if one expects a comparable degree of precision in the ascription. An explanation offered might stress elementary particles having wave properties in addition to their particle properties (Gamow 1962: 254–61). Thus, one cannot accurately model the properties of elementary particles on the properties of everyday objects. In summary, this way of reading the uncertainty principle claims that nature is fuzzy. (Call this the "fuzzy nature" interpretation.)

Of course, both of these versions of the uncertainty principle are here expressed extremely crudely. Nevertheless, the exposition should permit us to consider a determinist response to either of these positions, since the underlying structure of this variety of libertarianism in apparent even in this simplified account.

Is the uncertainty principle a red herring?

A determinist might respond to the suggestion that the first premise of his or her argument is shown to be false by considerations deriving from Heisenberg's uncertainty principle by raising a number of objections to either the formulation of such a response or to its impact on his or her (determinist) position.

First, the determinist might see such comments based on the uncertainty principle as a red herring. For even if one could not formulate causal laws for elementary particles (laws at the micro-level, as it were), surely it is possible to formulate such laws at the macro-level, like the level of human action. And the determinist would be happy once the existence of such causal laws were granted. As a parallel, the liquidity of water is not just a property of any of its particles: the particles themselves are not liquid. Nevertheless, liquidity is a property of water; a property of a collection of particles (Searle 1983: 265–8). And it is one that depends on the micro-properties of water. So a view on a larger scale than the particulate one is required. Thus even if, and this is certainly not conceded, there were no causal laws at the elementary particle level, this need not affect the determinist argument, in so far as that argument was directed at macro-events like human behaviour. For it is at the level of human behaviour that the determinist wishes to comment.

This objection is not decisive. The libertarians here urge that, since the causal laws will require analysis down to the micro-level, uncertainty considerations *do* preclude the writing of such causal laws: and hence the position does run counter to premise 1 of the determinist argument. Moreover, some of the attraction of determinism might disappear if its concerns were not both fundamental (in the ways that laws of physics can seem to be) and drawing support from scientific understanding (both its detail and its project: p. 58). However, determinism may still get underway if the distinction between levels that it might urge can indeed be sustained.

Second, the determinist might interrogate the notion of causation. One advantage these libertarians claimed for themselves over the Campbell position was that their views were built on science and hence did not fly in its face. The determinist might respond that they (the libertarians) have misinterpreted the nature of science here, since contemporary physicists continue to use the notion of causation – even physicists who accept Heisenberg's uncertainty principle! All the determinist needs, as an account of causation in his or her argument, is *whatever* picture of causation is urged by such physicists. So that, contrary to their hope, this second version of libertarianism fares no better than the first: it still flies in the face of the practice and the project of modern science.

As a third objection, this account seems to be undermining agency, rather than permitting it. For (as we saw when considering the Campbell position) free will defenders require reliable and explicable outcomes of actions: my deciding to do something "leading" to the occurrence of the something. But that kind of reliability might seem to be threatened if causal regularity is rejected in favour of mere probability. The determinist can then urge that whatever secures the reliability for the free will defender can also provide all the causal regularity he or she requires. This objection, put aside in the case of Campbell, has more "bite" here: the advocate of the uncertainty response to determinism must regard the behaviour of thrown dice too as not causally determined!

The determinists might also raise a fourth, related, objection. For their idea that physicists still use the notion of cause has, as it were, two dimensions. First, and minimally, the determinist can mean whatever the physicists mean (the objection just raised). But second, and maximally, adoption of this *powerful* a notion of freedom, such that all events where Heisenberg's uncertainty principle could be invoked were free, would have the consequence that human action was as "free" as, say, the movement of Halley's Comet, since it too is composed of elementary particles, etc. So this view makes human freedom of the same order as the "freedom" of the rest of the physical world. In this way, it undermines the contrast between agency and natural phenomena. Put roughly, this account concedes all that the determinist requires, by making humans as free as, say, billiard balls, and surely free will defenders required more to human freedom than this. Further, if accepted, this position proves too much: we would be obliged to attribute "freedom" to, for example, furniture, since furniture too is composed of elementary particles. This is clearly a very fundamental objection to this kind of libertarianism, suggesting that such a view does not (indeed, cannot) have an appropriate "fit" with the world of free action; that it does not provide a way to sustain the agency/happening contrast (Chapter 1, p. 1).

In reply, it might be suggested that, instead, these considerations succeed in showing us that the kinds of physical determinism stressed here are untenable. And since psychological determinism is an implausible thesis, as we have seen (Chapter 3, p. 46), that leaves no basis for the determinist argument. That is, advocates of this view might simply regard it as a negative thesis, dealing with the determinist argument; and then look for some other way to make out the agency/happening contrast.

To evaluate such a suggestion, we must enquire whether the objections to causal laws are really as strong as these advocates claim.

The uncertain issue of causality

The four objections raised in the previous section suggest that, as it were, this form of libertarianism has not got it right: that it does not really preclude the writing of causal laws, and that, if true, it would prove too much. A yet more fundamental objection must be differently formulated depending on which interpretation of the uncertainty principle (from the two sketched above, p. 62) one adopts. Different interpretations of Heisenberg's uncertainty principle leave one open to different but related forms of objection. I begin by assuming that the first interpretation, the "knowledge-to-humans" interpretation, is correct.

The final objection is that the uncertainty principle, according to this "knowledge-to-humans" interpretation, does not in fact do the job required. All it says is that the position and velocity of elementary particles are not accurately predictable *by humans*. This is not the same as urging that they are not predictable in principle. The determinist had already agreed that the practicalities of predicting may be permanently beyond human capacities: this did not affect his or her argument, since what was predictable in principle was predictable [KEY CASE 7], even if not by humans. So the determinist might feel that interpretation 1 of the uncertainty principle concedes all that is needed for the formulation of "in principle" laws.

That first interpretation, therefore, allows the possibility of such causal laws at the micro-level: it just denies that humans could ever formulate them. So the objection concedes all that the determinist requires. But such a line of objection could not go through on the second, "fuzzy nature" interpretation. For now it would be *in principle* impossible to formulate causal laws at the micro-level. Or so it might seem. We would no longer be discussing a limitation on the possibility of human knowledge: rather, the uncertainty, the "fuzziness", would be a feature of the world. In fact, a parallel objection can be formulated. By the first interpretation, the uncertainty principle did not deny that elementary particles have precise properties, merely that these properties could be precisely known by humans. Contrary to initial appearance, the second, "fuzzy nature" interpretation achieves nothing fundamentally different. Rather, it says that elementary particles have neither precise particle properties, nor precise wave properties. Thus, the difficulty lies in finding an intelligible model for the properties of the elementary particle: our everyday models, wave and particle, do not fit it exactly. To be clear, if elementary particles have precise properties, then causal laws can, in principle, be formulated for them, even though those causal laws would not resemble familiar wave laws or familiar particle laws. Nothing said here precludes the properties being precise (or non-fuzzy). Here the situation is strongly analogous to that arrived at on the first, "knowledge-to humans" interpretation: because of the unfamiliar character of the laws, humans would not *know* them – at least, no simple model of the event would follow from such laws. But there would still *be* laws. As before, the determinist can urge that the uncertainty principle provides no guarantee that actions are not predictable in principle.

Morals from the uncertainty considerations

What has this consideration of the underlying structures of the uncertainty based libertarianism taught us? First, any libertarianism that founds free action on the denial of causality must account for the reliability of the "outcomes" of action; that these are not merely random. But, if that can be achieved, there will be a degree of regularity from which a determinist might reconstruct (at the least) a Humean account of causation (Chapter 2, p. 29). Second, accounts that deny that *any* events have causes will owe an account of what distinguishes the behaviour of clouds from the behaviour of persons: if neither is causally determined, does that permit agency? Or does it preclude it?

More specifically, this account allows us to reconsider the nature of causal laws, and the detail of the explanatory project of science. We do not see explanatory discontinuities thrown up here. Campbell's position failed to located causal discontinuities where it required them (distinguishing actions done from duty from other actions) In a similar way, the suggestion that there is no difference here between the situations for persons and that for billiard balls means that we are as capable of finding causal laws for persons as we are for billiard balls; that causal laws apply equally to both, and with the same consequences (once considerations of complexity are put aside). So one might well conclude that causal laws just are the kinds of laws that can (in principle) be written to describe such physical systems. For that, more than anything else, is the project of scientific explanation.

This consideration has illustrated the major difficulties inherent in denying any explanatory force to causality; of denying that any events had causes in the relevant sense.

Conclusion

What have we got from our discussion of libertarianism in its two varieties? If the (determinist) objections to both versions strike us as compelling, two aspects of central importance here make it worth having considered libertarianism. First, principles such as "every event has a cause" are needed if we are to do justice to the project of science, and hence to allow the scientific study of "every event". For only in this way can we avoid flying in the face of science, as both the types of libertarianism considered here found, to their cost. If this point is acknowledged, the prospect for any acceptable libertarianism must be bleak.

Second, a place for causation is needed to provide a sense of order (as Hume, quoted earlier, suggested) for our descriptions and explanations. For the regularities and continuities within life and across lives are to be explained, as well as the differences. If, in two apparently similar situations, different outcomes result, we should conclude that the initial situations were not the same in every detail: different outcomes should be explained by locating differences within existing events. This is just the assumption the determinist makes. Moreover, we do not expect causal discontinuities in just some aspects of our lives. For our standard cases of free actions span a variety of human activities.

A final insight, concerning the scope of libertarianism, returns us to the idea of an "exact fit" on the everyday notion of free action. For Campbell's position (if successful) would unduly restrict the range of free actions, perhaps to moral actions only – certainly only those done from duty – while appeal to the uncertainty principle would unduly extend the range of free actions: the explanation of "freedom" would apply as well to the inanimate as to the animate world.

Compatibilism I:
5 the "utilitarian" position

Introduction

We concluded, in the previous chapter, that discussions of free will must begin from an acceptance of the thesis that every event has a cause; moreover, that the kinds of causes under discussion are those characterized by biophysics (from Chapter 3). Thus opponents of determinism are obliged to accept premise 1 of the determinist argument: every event does have a cause. What mileage, therefore, is there for the free will defender in denying premise 2 of that argument; that is, denying that actions are a kind of event? In the literature, there are two standard ways to articulate such a denial, both sometimes called "compatibilism", since causation is thought compatible with free action. The most usual (which I call the "two-language view") is considered in Chapter 6.[1] Another attempt to, as it were, *circumvent* the determinist position has no established name in the literature: I shall call it "the utilitarian position". That title is justified since (as with utilitarianism in moral philosophy[2]) the emphasis is on the consequences of actions. This position had, at one time, a number of adherents.[3] At its heart, it amounts to affirming the position of Dr Johnson: "Sir, we know our will is free, and there's an end on't" (quoted in Ayer 1954: 271).

Exposition of the utilitarian position

Of course, Johnson's blunt denial of the determinist conclusion cuts little ice with determinists, or even with those puzzled by the nature of free will. What is needed here is an articulated position endorsing free will and explaining how the determinist argument is to be combated. The utilitarian position involves making two points. First, a negative point: as we saw in Chapter 4, libertarians (for example, Campbell) and determinists assume that an action is either *free* or *caused*, but not both. This, say the utilitarians, is to confuse two distinctions:

- the distinction between caused and uncaused *events*, where "uncaused events" is an empty class – there just are no uncaused events;
- the distinction between constrained and free *actions*.

So the negative point denies that actions are a kind of event by asserting that the notion of an action is to be explained somehow differently from the notion of an event, so that the causality that (necessarily) attaches to events does not thereby attach to actions.

In granting that every event has a cause, this first contrast does not "fly in the face of science" (as Campbell's position did). Since the position goes on, in the second contrast, to discuss the nature of action from within such a contrast, I will not here explore this negative point explicitly (although a fuller discussion of this option would need to do so).

Second, there is a positive point, an attempt to articulate the free/constrained distinction for actions. For why should we accept the negative point, that there is a confusion of two distinctions, unless we can make out the second distinction in a clear and unambiguous fashion? The utilitarians begin by reminding us of characteristic cases of constraint: actions resulting from physical disorders, or drugs, and such like. Our central case has been the kleptomaniac, who ends up with a scarf taken from the department store [KEY CASE 2] but who, so free will defenders say, has not genuinely performed an action. The characteristic feature is that such cases do not imply moral responsibility on the part of the "agent". For these utilitarians, we first articulate the constrained actions, then all the rest (like walking across the room [KEY CASE 1]) are free actions.[4] Thus the central point here is that "If I am constrained, I do not act freely" (Ayer 1954: 278). Or, as Schlick puts it: "a man will be considered quite free and responsible if no . . . external compulsion is exerted upon him" (1966: 59). So that if I can identify cases where I am not constrained, those will be the free actions. Then a basis for deciding whether or not I am constrained must be sought: an action is free if unconstrained.

Of course, some actions may not fall smoothly into one category or the other. They might appear to be entailing moral responsibility at the time, and hence to be free, but later we might discover that they were not (say, acts done from false information, or genuine mistakes). In these cases, we might at the least *wish* to mitigate responsibility. Still, this possibility need not concern us. If there are some unconstrained actions (and also some constrained ones) the utilitarian will have begun articulating his or her case. And if we have such examples, we need to enquire how they differ.

Can a general difference between these two sorts of "action" be identified? In order that the utilitarian position be sustained, this contrast must be a reliable one: without it, the chief "prop" of the position is removed. (Notice that the utilitarian is much more concerned with actions that are constrained appropriately – for example, done under coercion, or duress, or stress – and hence the kind of determinism most readily combated will be psychological determinism, which we saw in Chapter 3 not to be the most challenging form of determinism.)

As implied above, utilitarians offer a simple way of drawing the distinction: one merely compares the deterrent value of threatening, blaming, or rational argument in general, on the agent: "It would be pointless to try to affect [the insane person or the kleptomaniac] . . . by means of promises or threats" (Schlick 1966: 61). The reason: precisely that he or she is not a free agent. As Schlick notes: "When a man is forced by threats to commit certain acts we do not blame him, but the one who held the pistol to his breast . . . this is the person . . . we must influence in order to prevent similar acts in the future" (1966: 61).

Conversely, then, when it is appropriate to blame him, he is acting freely. In this sense, as Schlick asserts, "Punishment is an educative measure" (1966: 60),[5] only appropriate to those who can be educated; that is, to agents. Then actions are not regarded as *free* where blaming, etc. will not tend to discourage the agent: for free choices, blaming, etc. *will* tend to affect the agent's conduct. For example, the kleptomaniac will not listen to rational argument, and neither will the person with a brain tumour [KEY CASE 6] (nor the man with a gun to his head, perhaps [KEY CASE 3]), a position clearly articulated by Nowell-Smith: "We might therefore say that moral traits of character are just those traits that are known to be amenable to praise or blame; and this would explain why we punish idle boys but not stupid ones, the sane but not the insane" (1954: 304).

The "utilitarian" position, then, turns the determinist argument on its head, urging that those events where praise or blame would be efficacious in altering the behaviour are free, rather than, as the determinist does, asking whether any behaviour *can* be affected by, for example, praise or blame. There seems something right in this. For we might well think that, across a range of human activity, praising activities will tend to make humans more likely to continue with them and censuring will have the opposite tendency.

An important question (postponed until p. 76–7) is whether the conclusion of this second, positive point is reached through a sound argument-form. Let us first consider the satisfactoriness of this as a position: what are its advantages?

Advantages to the utilitarian position

The utilitarian position concedes the determinist's first premise, that every event has a cause, while maintaining notions of moral responsibility, and indeed responsibility more generally. And, as we saw (Chapter 4), denial of that first premise will fly in the face of the project of science (and perhaps its achievements) and may endanger the reliability of "predictions" of what one will achieve oneself – how can I know what will occur, if causal connections cannot be relied upon?

Further, this position leaves the notion of choice where it intuitively is (as, perhaps, Campbell did not: Chapter 4, p. 60). What we would expect to be free actions tend to come out as free actions from this account. Indeed, the whole design of this account begins from those cases – for example our kleptomaniac [KEY CASE 2] – that we accept as *not* free. Notice, though, that the utilitarian account will make the kleptomaniac a person who performs constrained actions whereas (and perhaps more intuitively appropriate) the determinist treats the kleptomaniac as someone who does not perform actions at all, since the behaviour is explained purely causally.

Primarily, the utilitarian position is a kind of defusing of the debate, denying the central contrast on which the determinist was insisting: the contrast between the caused and the free. Instead, the determinist's mistake was diagnosed as a failure to attend to the free/constrained contrast for actions because he or she is concentrating too exclusively on the caused/uncaused contrast – and granting that the determinist is right (on that score): that there are no uncaused events!

Another kind of "utilitarian" position?

We might arrive at broadly the same conclusion in another way, beginning (Flew 1986: 79, Flew & Vesey 1987: 61 ff.) from the "fact" that human beings do ascribe responsibility to one another; do regard their actions as free. As Flew put it:

> since the meaning of "of his own freewill" can be taught by reference to such paradigm cases as that in which a man, under no social pressure, marries a girl he wants to marry . . . it cannot be right, on any grounds whatever, to say that no one ever acts of his own freewill.   (1956: 19)

So that:

> we have, in everyday life, criteria for determining whether an agent could have acted otherwise than he did, and those criteria determine the meaning of [the expression] "could have acted otherwise": to know the meaning of this phrase is simply to know how to apply those criteria.
> (van Inwagen 1982: 55[6])

The conclusion is that the notion of freedom is safeguarded by our sustained use of it.[7] So that the marriage between Joe and Jane is a free action *because* it is not an example of constraint: not a "shotgun" wedding, for example. On this variant, there is nothing more to its being free than its not being constrained: the question of causality (or otherwise) does not arise.

This version of the position effectively only offers what, above, was called the *negative point*: since we can talk plausibly about those actions that are constrained and about those that are free, a real distinction is being drawn: both sides of the contrast identify different conditions. Perhaps the cases mentioned show how the expressions "of his or her own free will" and "could have done otherwise" are used in English (we can readily imagine similar cases for other languages). But is what is implied if such a use of language is true? Is there free will, or free action? That cannot be established by pointing out that our common-sense understanding embodies a distinction between actions and happenings (see Chapter 1). As a general thesis, too much weight is placed on the vagaries of the development of English: surely there are, in English word-use, some contrasts that are merely apparent.[8] (We have only to reflect on what some dog- or cat-owners say of their pets to realize the problems inherent in inferring what is true of the world from what people sometimes (correctly) say.) So the mere fact that some event is *called* an example of *constraint* should not be taken to guarantee that there are events freely performed: that is, actions. Also, can we guarantee the stability of these contrasts between the constrained and the freely done in ways that this version of the position assumes? Even such utilitarians surely grant that there is some justice in recognizing, say, the powerful effects of an agent's home life; and therefore recognizing a mitigating force here: the event was not the free action we had thought it. Yet that accepts the fragility of the contrast between cases of constraint and non-constraint.

For our purposes, such worries as these can be put aside since, if we have a satisfactory way to articulate the free/constrained contrast (a way provided by the first version?), the worries disappears: if we do not, the inadequacies of that position may shed useful light on this one.

Disadvantages, problems, objections

Two major objections suggest that, at the very least, the utilitarian position will not succeed in answering the determinist case. First, the general principle invoked by the "utilitarians" for making the free/unfree distinction does not seem to work. Intuitively, more than just free agents are likely to be influenced by praise, and blame, and associated notions. So that filling the department store with very obvious security men might well deter our kleptomaniacs [KEY CASE 2] – our case of constrained behaviour, where notions of choice do not apply. Here, behaviour intuitively regarded as constrained will turn out, on the utilitarian position, to count as free.[9]

Similarly, a drug addict does (empirically) seem amenable to rational argument in at least some cases, whereas we withhold moral evaluation from his or her behaviour. It is far from obvious that the inefficacy of praise, blame, censure and the like will ultimately succeed in drawing the distinction between free actions and the rest in precisely the place that we wish. Indeed, when Ayer changed his mind about this, he offered as his reason the fact that "the boundaries of constraint are not at all easy to draw . . ." (Ayer 1963: 257: also quoted in Trusted 1984: 45). But, if this is so, it will be difficult to be confident either that the standard cases of freedom (beloved of free will defenders) are genuinely free or that some of the standard cases of constraint are not. In these ways, then, the utilitarian position may lack one of the advantages claimed for it (p. 72): it may draw some contrast between freedom and constraint, but fail to draw that contrast even roughly where it intuitively falls.

More damaging, the second objection urges that the utilitarian position gets everything upside-down. In the utilitarian position, free choice is made to rest on notions of *blame*, *reward*, and so on. For utilitarians, these notions are logically prior to free choice. This cannot be so. It is absurd to praise or blame someone unless he or she is a free agent. And this is the moral drawn from our cases of constraint: the kleptomaniac is not a free agent and therefore not appropriately praised and blamed – similarly the person with the brain tumour [KEY CASE 6]. As we put it in English law, persons are "not fit to plead" and therefore not culpable. The utilitarian position has the effect of turning this contrast on its head.

The upshot of these two objections, though, is that the "utilitarian position" does not succeed in putting aside our determinist argument. Its principal tool, the free/constrained distinction for actions, is not acceptable as it is there drawn: it fails to do the job, and also misconceives the relationship between responsibility and freedom. Were it correct, we should think of persons as free agents only if they were likely to be deterred by praise or blame; so that "hardened" criminals, undeterred by praise or blame, would turn out not to be criminals at all on this account. Such a conflict with our established common-sense suggests that this position is misconceived.

These difficulties have focused on the positive thesis of our utilitarian position, finding it wanting. But what of our "second" version, which simply urged the negative thesis? Its "argument" reminded us that we use the free/constrained contrast unproblematically in a large number of cases, even if there were a few tricky borderlines; and it implicitly suggested that (in disputing the application of the term "free", or in beginning from cases of acknowledged constraint) the determinist was importing the very contrasts that were then disputed. Its difficulty is that, to the determinist, it simply consists in begging the question against him: assuming that the common-sense contrasts are sound, when the determinist has given (what free will defenders should (see Chapter 3, p. 39) see as) *arguments* to the contrary. For, without a principled basis from which the free/constrained contrast may be drawn, the determinist has no motivation to accept these conclusions.

Finally, and as a partial aside, we can profitably return to a question raised earlier. The utilitarian conclusion cannot be sustained: but was the argument by which the positive point (the free/constrained distinction as depending on responsibility) was introduced a sound one? That its conclusion has been rejected will incline us towards a negative answer: but where exactly was the problem?

This argument begins, uncontentiously, with the thought, as we might put it, that only when a person is free can we blame him or her. This seems to say that if we can blame, say, *Joe* for the barn's catching fire, it follows that he is a free agent. This is rather misleading: for can we blame him? Certainly we can say words of blame, as we do too, for instance, regarding the behaviour of domestic pets! Here, we are not really blaming the pets, but hoping that (for instance) the tone of voice will operate causally to preclude a repetition of whatever event. No, the issue is not whether or not we can blame *Joe* (where this means, roughly, "utter words of blame"), but whether or not we *should* do so.

Now, that way of putting the issue can mislead too; for it asks if our blaming him has any point. But asking about "any point" in doing something is sometimes asking whether it is efficacious and sometimes asking if it is appropriate. Clearly, it is only appropriate to blame *Joe* if he is an agent (and if he is guilty!). So we cannot resolve the question of appropriateness prior to being clear on the issue of Joe's being (or not being) an agent. (That was our conclusion above: that the utilitarian position turns on their heads the common-sense contrasts that free will defenders value.) Yet our utilitarians read the question as asking about the efficacy of blaming. There is a general pattern of explanation here. For utilitarians, the (moral) goodness of an action is to be explained in terms of that action's maximizing (what they would call) *utility*: that is, of the actions turning out, on balance, to have more positive consequences than other courses of action (or inaction), assuming that some "measure" of utility is available (in principle[10]). So that, in general, the characteristics of actions are understood by utilitarians in terms of their (possible) consequences; and the agent's "motivation" too is understood in terms of the action's consequences: my desire to do good is a desire to perform actions that maximize utility. Now, if this were in general the right way to think about actions, the nature of my action (in our case, as free) would be explicable in terms of the changing circumstances in which the utility calculations might come out differently. Put bluntly, this way of thinking always pays attention to the external circumstances in explaining agent-motivation. Perhaps its failure here may make us reconsider it more generally, as an account of the motivation of action (Dancy 1993: esp. 3–4).

Conclusion

The utilitarian position shows that we cannot begin from our "certainty" in our own freedom (and hence our own responsibility) as Dr Johnson did in the passage quoted (p. 69). To begin from a sense of ourselves as moral agents is just to *assume* the freedom of the will. Faced with the determinism argument to the contrary, such an assumption is simply unwarranted: we need an argument for free will, not merely its assertion.

   The determinist has so far been fought on his or her own ground, as it were. Both Campbell and those employing the uncertainty principle (Chapter 4) conceded the incompatibility of causal continuity and free will; we have seen the unprofitability of such a line. Moreover the utilitarians (having conceded the need for causal continuity) tried to distinguish between types of causation, for example those that permit freedom of action and those that do not. But this too looks unpromising. What is needed, it seems, is a position that does not meet the determinist on his or her own ground. It is to such a position, still denying the incompatibility of free will and causality, that we now turn.

Compatibilism II:
6 the two-language view

Introduction

In Chapter 5 we saw the unsatisfactory character of disputing the truth of premise 2 of the determinist argument, the premise stating that actions are a kind of event, by urging, simply, that actions differed from events because actions brought with them notions of responsibility in ways in which event-descriptions did not. Another, more standard, way of attempting to deny the truth of premise 2 of that argument is sometimes called "compatibilism" or "reconciliationism" or even "soft determinism". None of these names is entirely happy, since each suggests only some aspect of the position named, rather than getting to its heart. Here is one place our characterization of determinism can seem important: theorists who think universal causation is compatible with action (for instance, Dennett 1984; Fischer 1994) have sometimes called themselves *determinists*, but of some special kind: say, soft determinists.[1] In my view, they are free will defenders since, for them, the determinist's conclusion does not follow from his or her first premise alone. And the standard names have all been associated with some particular theorist's view.[2] So I prefer a neutral name, and hence call this the "two-language" view.

The burden of this position is the logical independence of two ways of describing and explaining occurrences (the "language" of causes and the "language" of action[3]) so that no statement in the "language" of causes can entail a statement of choice. This undermines premise 2 of the determinist argument since what the determinist means by the term "event" (in effect, explained in premise 1 of his or her argument) involves event-description being essentially causal. Denying that causal descriptions may appropriately be joined with action descriptions is therefore a way of saying that actions are indeed *not* a kind of event. And even if action-explanations themselves operated causally (as urged by, say, Davidson 1980; Audi 1993), those action-explanations are still viewed as importantly different from event-explanations: so I shall continue to characterize only the event descriptions (and not the action descriptions) as the "language" of causes.[4]

In this position, then, there are two distinct kinds of explanation and description (two distinct "languages"). And, since an event may not be simultaneously described in both ways,[5] an occurrence at any one time must be seen as either an event or an action but not both. (Yet is just one thing going on here, as the term "occurrence" might suggest? As we will see, that will turn out to be an important issue (Chapter 8, p. 119). There is only *one* set of bodily movements: to this degree, there is one causal story, and therefore some sense of "one happening".[6]) According to the two-language view, identifying two distinct kinds of explanations is denying that actions (which must be described using one kind of explanatory framework) are a species of event, since events must be described using the other kind.

Defenders of this position must answer two important questions. They must, first, explain how these kinds of explanation and description are indeed *distinct*, for only a genuine difference here will make the position plausible. Second, they must explain why both kinds of explanation and description are *necessary*. A determinist, after all, might acknowledge that, in everyday life, both causal description and action description are *used*: his or her point will be simply that we do not need to do so, and further that there is something misleading about doing so, given that the notion of choice has no application. So, to combat that position, defenders of the two-language view must show not simply that there are two distinct kinds of explanation and description, but that the richness of human life can only be captured by using both.

It is tempting to look for descriptions of all human behaviour in the same terms used to describe the behaviour of other things, like shoes and ships and sealing wax: the terms used there are causal. So we might look for neurophysiological causes (or causes at the level of biophysics) with bodily movements as their events: the determinist would surely approve such description, as describing one segment of the causal chain at least. However, adopting this course seems disastrous, because the causal mode does no justice to the context of an action, as we shall see.

Two distinct ways of describing and explaining.

We begin with some standard examples of explanation and description of occurrences using, first, the "language" of action and, second, the "language" of causes.

> 1A I intended to go to London yesterday
> I made up my mind to . . .
> 1B Movement of rock caused the earthquake.
> The sudden drop in temperature caused the rain storm.
> 2A I went to London yesterday.
> I have/I will . . .
> 2B The earthquake occurred.
> The rainstorm occurred.

No proposition in list 1A (which are statements giving reasons) entails[7] a proposition in list 2A. I may intend to go to London without going; I may decide to do something and still not do it.

Is there an analogue for causal statements? Consider the causal statements[8] of group B: a proposition in list 1B does entail a proposition in list 2B. If it is true that the movement of rock caused the earthquake then it is true that the earthquake occurred. One thing cannot cause another without the second occurring. How are we to characterize this difference? Introducing some terminology, we can say that the causal descriptions allow for the substitution of true descriptions with *truth being preserved*.[9] For example, taking a rainstorm to be a sudden precipitation of H_2O, we might replace the expression "the rainstorm" in B with the expression "the sudden precipitation of H_2O". Then if it were *true* that the sudden drop in temperature caused the rainstorm, it would definitely be true that the sudden drop in temperature caused the precipitation of H_2O. Equally, if it were false that the sudden drop in temperature caused the rainstorm, it would be equally false that the sudden drop in temperature caused the precipitation of H_2O: if one of these is true, the other must be. As philosophers say, they have the same *truth value*.

Applying the same technique to examples in A, since London is the capital city of England, we might make that substitution. If I intended to go to London yesterday, is it automatically true that I intended to go to the capital city of England yesterday? No. The first of these could be true and the second still false. I might (for instance) believe that London is not the capital city, and what I can genuinely intend here reflects that belief. So I might intend to go to London without intending to go to the capital city. (If asked, I would truthfully deny I was going to the capital.) Or so it seems. Here, our two kinds of explanations work differently. Causal explanation permits substitution *preserving truth*, while explanation in terms of reasons does not guarantee that substitution will *preserve truth*. Now consider some further examples.

> C I shall go to the football match because I enjoy football. Smith gave to Oxfam because Oxfam is helping the needy.

Compare this list with a slight rearrangement of list B, along the following lines.

B (revised) The earthquake occurred because of the movement of rock. The rainstorm occurred because of the sudden drop in temperature.

Contrasting these two cases, we can pick out the following differences:

- **Causes temporally precede effects**
  Causes (as in list B) either temporally precede or occur at the same time as their effects: the movement of rock occurred before or at the same time as the earthquake. But this is not so with a reason. Reasons don't seem to be in time at all. When *exactly* is it that I enjoy football? Certainly, when I am playing it or watching it, I may be actively enjoying it; but surely it is true of me (at any time) that I enjoy football. A reason is (roughly) a statement that, if true, justifies what it is a reason for.

- **Reasons are logical relations**

  Reasons justify: they are good or bad, better or worse (see White 1968: 17), and action need have no reason (something someone just does). But causes cannot be good or bad – the outcome either is caused in that way or it is not. Moreover, causes do not justify, and (here we agree with the determinist) all events have causes.

  The relationship between reason, and what is a reason for, is a logical relationship. But what *causes* what depends on the way the world is and hence is described (ultimately) by the laws of science. Logic (we say) allows anything to cause anything, so the movement of rock could have caused any old thing: indeed, anything can cause anything (given different scientific laws). But not anything can be *reason* for anything – for certain actions, it is absurd to give certain things as reasons. Suppose someone urged, as a reason for murdering his or her wife, that she could not cook. We can more or less understand how this might come about (which does not make it a genuine justification, of course). We can (almost) see how the events are related – even if this seems a totally inappropriate reaction. But how about, as a reason for murdering one's wife, "because tomorrow is Tuesday"? As it stands, this is absurd. No doubt some context (say a religious one) might be given, welding it to some notion of what is important. But not easily. So the relation of being a reason does not function like causation (or so it seems).

- **"In order to . . ."**

  Reason-type explanation often asks for purposes or motives; the "because" can be replaced by "in order to". It makes sense to say, "Smith gave to Oxfam in order to help the needy", but not "there was a drop in temperature in order to . . .". Why did the earthquake occur? "In order to . . .": well, what? This kind of explanation, sometimes called "teleological",[10] simply does not fit with causal accounts.[11]

- **Inexorability of causes**

  One thing cannot be a *cause* of another without the second happening (as we noted above). So the truth of the items in list lB guarantees the truth of the corresponding items in list 2B. As we saw, this guarantee does not hold for reasons.

- Knowing causes vs. knowing reasons
  At the least I do not typically know the causes of my behaviour, conceived as changes in my neurophysiology or biochemistry. Yet it must be at least conceivable that I can know my own reasons, even if I cannot always articulate them.

Here, then, are some features of the causal "language", not shared or guaranteed by the reasons "language". Such considerations suggest that causal explanation is importantly different from explanation via reasons or choices. If this is so, we cannot expect to "translate" one kind of explanation into the other without "remainder"; that is, without leaving something out. Yet that is precisely what the second premise of the determinist argument asks us to do (Chapter 2, p. 21), for it treats a statement about actions (explained via the "language" of action) as equivalent to a statement about events (explained causally): it says that actions are one kind of event.

The importance of context

If those considerations suggest that the "language" of causes operates differently from the "language" of reasons or choice, defenders of the two-language view must still show that both kinds of explanation are *necessary*: that a complete causal account does not imply an action account, nor vice versa. For then we cannot, as the determinists think, reduce action accounts to causal accounts without losing something.

Consider, first, formal procedures (Wilkerson 1974: 133–9), where characterizing an activity requires reference (explicitly or implicitly) to the *rules* that govern whatever type of activity it is. For formal procedures – voting, cheque-signing, marriage – the rules, the context, must be mentioned if the procedures are to be adequately characterized. As Wilkerson (1974: 133) comments, to describe a man as picking up pieces of paper from a wooden desk is not to offer a *poor* description of his visit to the bank: rather, one is simply not describing his withdrawing money at all, any more than talking of the redistribution of elaborately carved pieces of wood on a chequered surface is really talking about chess. (Indeed, puzzles about such formal activities can often be clarified by appeal to the analogy with games such as chess.) An account that did justice to the idea of *cashing a cheque* would explain about money, about the role of banks (for example, that they do not just keep each person's money in a separate shoe-box), and perhaps about world banking. Since a characterization of what occurred must refer to these rules, a causal account cannot be adequate, since those rules will relate to social interaction rather than to the working-out of physical processes. In this way, the other account would not be just an *elaboration* of the causal story, for failing to mention the rules is not describing voting, or the signing of cheques, at all.

Of course, these rules would not typically be mentioned explicitly. In day-to-day life in the Western world, cheque-signing is so embedded, its rules sufficiently taken-for-granted, that perhaps it no longer comes into the formal category there, but counts as informal. Equally, this is not so for the larger proportion of the world's population: it does draw on an explicit set of formal "rules". Yet it illustrates the inter-connectedness of these ideas.

Consider [KEY CASE 9] (McFee 1992: 53) an intelligent, English-speaking Martian who arrives at a church on a Saturday afternoon. Since she is a being of superior powers, she knows perfectly well the causal stories involved in the event she witnesses – what free will defenders would speak of as three persons talking together. Moreover, the Martian perfectly well understands the words being uttered. However, surely she does not understand the action being performed, the action of marrying, unless she also knows broadly the *rules* that permit this discussion among persons to count as a marriage, and moreover at least some of what the notion of marriage amounts to; say, in terms of property rights or responsibilities. But our case is yet clearer if we imagine the same Martian arriving at the church on the Thursday evening, when she would see the same group of people talking together, uttering the same words, and absolutely nothing would follow from it; for this would be the rehearsal.

Notice, first, that without appeal to the nexus of rules surrounding the concept of marriage, any description or explanation of the event offered by the Martian will be inadequate. (For her, the same explanation would apply to marriage and to rehearsal.) So both causal explanation and others are necessary. Second, although the rules provide a context to the happening, that context is not solely provided (does not solely consist in) either the buildings or the collections of words. Such a case suggests that, for such formal activities, one is not describing the action *at all* unless reference is made (perhaps implicitly) to the rules governing that activity.

Now, consider informal activities: here too the idea of activities as *rule-governed* has a place; situations where roles (for example, as parent or as teacher) or conventions are important in characterizing what occurred, and, therefore, in explaining it. Can we describe purely causally the teacher dressing prior to coming to teach? A causal description of the body, the garments, the relevant changes in the brain and central nervous system, and so on, is possible. But that does not really characterize the occurrence, for that occurrence is surrounded by "rules", conventions and roles. For example, even in a school with no dress code, teachers are expected to wear something: teaching in the nude is (typically) inappropriate, although no explicit school rule forbids it. (In a more litigious future, one will!) And the point is not purely aesthetic, nor one on which teachers or pupils are typically asked to vote (although they might be). Equally, one fails in one's teacherly role by arriving at class nude: and that fact is surely important in any explanation of one's arriving there clothed. This point suggests that everyday action cannot always be adequately described without going beyond causal descriptions. The context supplies constraints on what can occur, although perhaps none could be explicitly stated as rules.

How do we explain (where this means "explain away") actions? Often this asks for the motive, the intention, the reason *behind* the action (Taylor 1964: 36). Yet we have seen that reason-type explanation is not like cause-type explanation, even though both answer questions beginning "Why did it happen?" by saying "Because . . ."; and even though the word "reason" is sometimes used when we mean "cause", as in "What is the reason for the car breaking down?" (In a spy thriller, for example, there might even be a reason: to delay the villain while the hero gets there, or to allow a rendezvous, or something. The breakdown was deliberate – but not on the car's part!)

In general, then, the social character of action is being stressed. But what is social about, say, you taking a bath (Doyal and Harris 1986: 73)? You are not interacting with anyone. You decide what soap to use, how hot to make the water, how long to soak, and so on (at least, within limits). So where does society enter the picture?

First, individuals learn how to act from other individuals, so I have learned that make of soap and length of soak are things to consider; second, information about social institutions must be incorporated into any explanation of individual action, if it is to be seen as action, explaining what I did and why.

Most human actions are *context-dependent* in just this way. Suppose I raise my arm [KEY CASE 10], just one causal story describing this event in terms of changes in my central nervous system, my musculature and so forth. Depending on the context, I may be exercising my muscles, signalling, pointing, warding off a blow, buying a table in an auction, buying a chair in an auction, asking to leave the room, or even giving an example in a philosophy talk. But all these actions involve the same cause-and-effect story, the same changes in my muscles and my central nervous system or whatever (as we specified in setting up the case). So here the same causal story is told of different human actions. If this is possible, even a complete causal account will not imply the action account.

But equally, a different causal story can also be told of one and the same action. Consider my offending a colleague [KEY CASE 11]: I might do this in a variety of ways: for example, by talking to him (with one causal story) or by not talking to him (another causal story), or by hitting him (another story). I might offend him by kicking his dog, but also by not sending him a Christmas card; so we could not readily provide a causal account showing in what the action consists. This is especially difficult for omissions. And all (or almost all) human action, when viewed *as* human action, is of this context-dependent sort.

These two cases display the impossibility of moving seamlessly from action-description to causal description, or vice versa.

This section, then, has filled in the sense in which, relative to corresponding movement-descriptions, action-descriptions cannot be translated "without remainder": characterizing an action in terms of the movements comprising it always omits something fundamental, namely, precisely which action is being performed. For characterizing that action requires its location in a background of social understandings that determine its "context": the nexus of "rules" (formal and informal) noted above. In this sense, as the two-language theorist urges, movement-descriptions are not equivalent to the corresponding action-description.

The normativity of action

One further characteristic of action-descriptions differentiates them from causal descriptions (see McFee 1992: 52–4). To introduce the point, a useful comparison is with the game of chess, for the nexus of rules operative there resembles that implicit in context-dependent action. Here, one might ask, first, whether the particular movement of a piece is actually a legitimate move in chess: I have moved my bishop one square, but is this permitted by the rules? If it is, perhaps the piece still arrived there by luck: that the movement was in accordance with the rule without depending on the rule. For example, a seal might be trained to push chess pieces around, and the pieces as pushed by the seal indeed correspond to legitimate moves in chess: but no seal was (yet?) playing chess. So our first contrast is between legitimate and non-legitimate moves.

But a second contrast is between good and bad moves. While the bishop may perfectly legitimately be placed on this square, this may be a bad move, causing me to lose the game. It might even be *thought* a bad move but turn out, on analysis, to have been a good one. This second feature, that moves in chess can be good or bad, introduces the normativity of action. The behaviour of trained seals (noted above) might accord with a certain rule, but lack the relevant rule-following characteristic of normativity: the seals did not do it because of the rule! Therefore it would be misleading to think of the seals as genuinely *doing* the thing (say, playing Bluebells of Scotland on cycle horns). Rather, the seal behaves in ways that, if done by humans, would amount to performing that action. So (a) rule-governed-ness and (b) normativity are two aspects of the context-dependence characteristic of human action.

To consider the relationship between normativity and context, recognize that the action of, for example, naming a ship can backfire in a number of different ways. For example, if ship-naming required that, while breaking a bottle over the ship, the namer say, "I hereby name this ship   ." followed by the name of the ship, and the namer, for instance, Her Majesty The Queen, said something other than the intended name of the ship (in a television advertisement, a namer said, "That's a bottle of good champagne being wasted"), the ship would indeed be named, but with the wrong name. If instead the namer uttered some other formula while breaking the bottle – for instance, "I baptise this ship . . ." – the ship would not be named: the right person would have said the wrong words, and hence not have performed the action of naming the ship. Equally if I, who has no business naming ships, break the bottle saying, "I hereby name this ship . . ." (and even if I then utter the name chosen for the ship), that ship is not named: the right "behaviour" has not amounted to the right action, since I am not an appropriate namer of ships.

The cases in this section and the previous one illustrate both that something will be omitted in any "translation" of action-stories into causal ones and that the action-stories might reasonably be thought to pick out important features of the world.

Complete statement of the two-language view.

A blunt summary of the two-language view may be useful, to show precisely what is urged. It might run roughly as follows.

1. There is a fundamental logical difference between the "language" of causes and the "language" of action, therefore they are logically independent.

2. The determinist tries to force us to use merely the "language" of causes and not the "language" of action, which carries with it talk of moral responsibility and freedom, by reducing actions to events (in premise 2 of his or her argument).

3. But no statement (or set of statements) about causes can entail any statements describing actions as such (from 1 above).

4. So the determinist's premise that "every event has a cause" does not entail the determinist conclusion that the "language" of action is vacuous, spurious or whatever: contrary to the determinist view, actions are not a kind of event.

5. The "language" of action and the "language" of causes are merely two different ways of describing the world. Neither is superior to the other, neither rules-out the other.

So why have two "languages" at all? Because we have two purposes. When doing science, we want (roughly) a third-person view of the world (Williams 1985: 139; Nagel 1986: 3–4), so we employ the "language" of causes. And we describe one another in causal terms, as our doctors sometimes do, when a detached, third-person view is required. But choosing between alternatives or evaluating behaviour requires a personal view of the world, and so we employ the "language" of action, and talk about reasons, choices, motives, intentions, responsibilities and the like.

Insights from the two-language view.

Before addressing the adequacy of the two-language view as a response to determinism (pp. 92–7), consider some of its insights, since we may adopt these even if it has not adequately dealt with the determinist challenge. A first major insight comes from acceptance of the difference between explanation in terms of reasons and explanation in terms of causes: we must be clear whether we are offering *reason-type* description and explanation of a piece of human behaviour or *movement-type* causal description or explanation. And that means being clear about the kind of question one is answering. A physician will typically (appropriately) regard (some) other humans in causal terms, as broken mechanisms. But providing causal explanations of events is adopting a detached viewpoint incompatible with seeing those events as involving human beings (because agency will have no place in it). This point is important, of course, for the variety of theorists who attempt to describe or explain human events in solely causal terms: doing this commits one to the determinist conclusion, at least if no further refutation of determinism is introduced.

A second insight concerns the place of context: in different contexts, the very same sequence of movements could be different actions. For example [KEY CASE 10], in the auction room, the movement of my arm going up could be the action of buying a table. In a classroom, that very same sequence of movements, with the same causal description, perhaps, might be the action of asking to leave the room. So characterizing the action requires taking into account the *description under which* that action was intentional, and bearing in mind the context. Of course, this is not simply equivalent to accepting the description the agent might offer. For, and notoriously, agents can be wrong as to their intentions. But it does mean that certain descriptions will be appropriate ones in that context and others not. Suppose that Mary is to go out with John, who is the second tallest man in London. On the day of their date, Mary is not performing the action of going out with the second tallest man in London, even though it is true that she is going out with the second tallest man in London. For the action is not intentional under that description. So, seeking to characterize what is going on, one must look for the description under which the action is intentional or deliberate.

Finding the two-language view insightful can explain an oddity in determinism (noted in Chapter 2, p. 33): that being a determinist was a thankless task. For the determinist restricts himself to the "language" of causes when, as noted, viewing human activity as truly human requires the "language" of action. (But our determinist will simply reply that he has shown the emptiness of the "language" of action.)

As a third insight, notice how the two-language view works against the worship of measurement and of a crude view of science. For it affirms that action-descriptions are genuine or real descriptions, picking out features of the world; features not amenable to the causal description commonly favoured by science. In a familiar example [KEY CASE 12] (Best 1974: 64), asked by his wife why he is drunk, the husband giving the causal answer, "Because I have so many milligrams of alcohol per millilitre of blood" (or even "Because I drank ten pints of beer") simply fails to answer the asked question. Of course, what he says is true (even quantifiable), but without addressing what the wife wants to know. Other questions might be asked in that same form of words. The wife wants an action-type answer: "I have been celebrating my promotion"; or "I was drowning my sorrows at being fired", for example. Here the two-language view identifies a major flaw in the determinist's picture of the world. The determinist rightly assumes that everything in the world can be examined scientifically, without anything being left out. For physics examines all the fundamental particles and forces in the universe, and human bodies are composed of some of these. But the determinist concludes that this is the *only* sort of acceptable examination (Best 1978: 70), a conclusion undermined by the two-language view. Since action-description is legitimate, there are *other* acceptable ways of describing facts about the world.

The strategy of the two-language view, then, urges that the determinist argument is not compelling because its second premise is false: actions are not a kind of event. Rather, actions can only be characterized using concepts from the "language" of action: and this way of characterizing behaviour brings with it the common-sense contrasts identified in Chapter 1. Failing to employ the "language" of action here means that the behaviour was not adequately characterized at all. So there can be no "reduction" of action-description to movement-description (see Chapter 1) without remainder. On the contrary, something crucial would necessarily be left out in such a "translation". If true, this means that action-description of what occurred is not simply dispensable: hence actions are not a species of event. Instead, each must be thought of differently.

Adopting this position offers some sizeable insights. But how satisfactory an answer to the determinist is this? To decide, we must consider (at least) three linked objections that the determinist might make to the two-language view.

Criticism – independence?

The first objection concerns the supposed logical independence of the two "languages". Here the determinist, noting an oddity of the two-language view, initially urges that the independence of these two sorts of descriptions and explanations is not as absolute as its advocates assume. For many simple activities, there is a causal story largely (perhaps exclusively) correlated with an action description. For example, if John is smoking a cigarette, certain causal interactions between John and the cigarette are taking place. A defender of the two-language view might register that there is no unique causal story here: a cigarette holder or hookah might transform the causal description. Still, this comment suggests that the two-language view has over-stated its case.

But the notion of independence here might be assailed in another and more important way. For the determinist reminds the defender of the two-language view that, in certain crucial cases (for example, the kleptomaniac [KEY CASE 2]), even free will defenders allow conflict between these supposedly "logically independent" ways of describing and explaining. When descriptions as *theft* (action-description) or as *kleptomania* (causal-description) competed, the causal description, which the determinist prefers, won through. Even free will defenders grant that, when kleptomania (rather than theft) was the appropriate characterization, the action-description (theft) was somehow superseded or defeated, and so the behaviour was not theft. "What is the relevant difference in other cases?", the determinist asks rhetorically. For he believes that all cases are relevantly similar: just as the kleptomaniac "could not do otherwise" than take the scarf from the department store because his or her actions were causally determined, so the "actions" of the rest of us are causally determined too.

Cases of constrained behaviour are crucial to free will defenders because, like the ones dear to our hearts, they involve the allocation of rights and responsibilities, of praise and blame. Perhaps some concepts describing actions could be explained without appeal to genuine choice and such like – concepts which can be given a reductive analysis (see below). But concepts relevant in morality, for example, do not fall into this category. So the defender of the two-language view may have characterized some kind of difference between two ways of explaining and describing, but he or she has not (yet) generated the kind of logical independence required to undermine determinism.

Criticism – adequacy?

A second problem the determinist might raise concerns the two-language view's adequacy: does it really refute the determinist argument? For the two-language view, only actions are free; but what are actions? In particular, actions typically involve movements of the body (of one sort or another); as buying the table in the auction [KEY CASE 10] was "composed" of my arm going up, and various movements of other objects. So an occurrence described as an action has no laws governing it in the way in which (so the determinist urged) there are causal laws. But that occurrence can also be described in causal terms, and then it has law-governed characteristics.

Such a position can produce a reductive account of choice [KEY CASE 13]. Suppose I approach the food in a self-service restaurant, and pick up a salad from a counter that also contains hot meals: have I not thereby chosen the salad (perhaps chosen it instead of the hot meal)? To choose here is just to take one option when faced with "alternatives": to choose *from* those "alternatives". And (says the two-language view) this choice is not predictable, even in principle, since there are no genuine laws for actions. This is a reductive account of choice in that it treats choosing as nothing but reaching out for one thing in the face of "alternatives": we confuse ourselves by giving too much attention to (the appearance of) a complicated weighing of relative values as a prelude to, or ingredient of, choosing.

The determinist then reminds us of the limited sense in which these really were alternatives. For it is agreed on both sides that the movements of my body are causally necessitated. Given the relevant causal history, it was inevitable that my arm should have extended in just such a way, that my fingers should have closed, and so on. Thus the salad will have ended up grasped in my hand. And if this is not exactly my action having been *determined*, the difference looks fairly slight.

First, although we might be unhappy with this sort of a reductive account of choice, suppose we go along with it, for the moment. It then permits us to see many everyday occurrences as examples of choice, and hence as free: for example, my choosing to walk across the room [KEY CASE 1]. And an important constraint on accounts of free action was that such everyday actions turn out to be free.

But, second, whatever the general plausibility of the two-language view, a reductive account of choice seems inadequate for moral choices, or, more generally, choices where responsibility is involved. For the idea of responsibility implies persons responsible (as agents) for any actions they perform, and thereby due any praise or blame attaching to those actions (they are to be held responsible). And a key notion of morality is that each of us should "get what we deserve".[12] Let us call the concepts used to ascribe responsibility (etc.) "desert concepts", since they relate to persons getting what they deserve. Such concepts centrally include the kinds of commendation or praise and the kinds of blame that attach to humans as agents, or as originators of "actions"; and might extend to notions of compensation or reparation for injury and to feelings of gratitude or resentment. We are familiar with examples [KEY CASES 4–6] where *responsibility* is fundamental.[13]

Yet can one deserve praise or blame when the outcome does not depend on choices made or decisions taken? Surely not. A presupposition that I "could have done otherwise" than I did seems built in (contrast Chapter 7), for the desert concepts to have genuine application in my case. If the outcome did not depend on, say, decisions I took or actions I initiated, I cannot deserve any praise or blame accruing to that outcome. Thus, merely reductive accounts of choice [KEY CASE 13], which can give no substantial sense to the idea of my "doing otherwise", will not save these concepts so dear to the heart of free will defenders. Therefore, the determinist views the two-language view as doomed to failure as a free will defence: adopting its conclusions cannot preserve the very notions most crucial for free will defenders.

Criticism – causal necessity?

But has the two-language view really achieved anything towards the refutation of determinism? To reply fully, we should first be clearer about the relation of the reductive view of choice (described above: p. 93) to the two-language view: does it follow automatically? Might other accounts of choice, consistent with the two-language view, be possible here? For another account of choice might offer a view of actions giving a role in the occurrence of that action to, say, rational considerations conceived of as *other than* counter-causal. Yet no such alternative account seems obvious, since it must both accommodate the causal forces operative on the action ("every event has a cause") and give some role to rationality.

Suppose the reductive account of choice follows from the two-language view. Now the determinist can formulate the major objection to this view: namely, that a reductive view of choice concedes what is essential for the determinist's conclusion, conceding the inevitability of that person ending up with, say, that cheese salad [KEY CASE 13].

Thus, this third objection generalizes from the second, by challenging the satisfactoriness of a reductive account of choice as a general tool against determinism. If the causal account of an event is sometimes accepted, causal necessity is at work. We imagine a choice (for example, in the case of the auction) involving whether or not I buy the table [KEY CASE 10]. But if my arm will go up at a certain moment during that auction, because of the causal forces, I will end up buying the table; or, at the least, a lot of explaining is required to avoid that conclusion. After all, my bodily movements have a causal story; regarded simply as bodily events (rather than as actions), causal necessity applies (as the two-language view concedes). So, if an auction is taking place on Tuesday afternoon, at 3.30 p.m., and given simply the bodily movement of my arm going up at that time (where a causal story can be given), I will buy whatever is then for sale (assuming this to be the final "bid"): if it were the table, I would (inevitably) buy the table.

So, for all its power and persuasiveness, the two-language view has not penetrated the final veils of this mystery: since a causal description still applied, if it were still true, then the determinist would be right; and all talk of choosing to do this or that would be, as it were, icing on the cake. To recall an earlier case (p. 90), perhaps Mary's action was not intentional *under the description* "going out with the second tallest man in London". None the less she was going out with the second tallest man in London, whether she liked it or not, or chose it or not.

To put the objection here a little more formally, suppose the determinist accepts, for the moment, that the two-language view undermines premise 2 of his or her argument: actions are not a kind of event. None the less, every action (even omissions) will involve some sequence of bodily movement on the part of some human being (or beings). So there will be a causal story underlying the happening, which is that action. Perhaps, viewed as action, the event is not causally determined (this is granted for the sake of argument): but what happened can *also* be viewed as an event. Viewed that way, it is causally determined. Thus the determinist might redraft his or her argument, focusing no longer on actions but on the bodily movements that underlie them: he or she might, as a second premise, urge that some set of bodily motions comprise any action (even an omission). Then the bodily motions comprising a certain action were caused (even if it were conceded that the action was not). A suitably transposed version of the fourth premise of the determinist argument would introduce the causal necessity of such bodily motions, given their causal antecedents. From there, the spuriousness of the idea of choice still follows: the bodily movements could not have been other than they were, so they were not chosen among some genuine alternatives.

Consider again my arm going up at 3.30 p.m. on a Tuesday afternoon [KEY CASE 10]. The two-language view, if accepted, has guaranteed that we cannot move seamlessly from even a complete knowledge of the causal description to recognizing what action description applies. So we cannot be sure whether I am buying a table in an auction or buying a chair in an auction. But I will be buying whatever is for sale in the auction at half past three. So the determinist's argument will conclude that the "language" of action is indeed spurious since there are no genuinely alternative outcomes at a particular time and place, at least when those outcomes are viewed as bodily movements. Thus the two-language account has not genuinely made room for choice, but only for the feeling of choice.

Of course, this example leaves out the causal chain that leads up to the bodily event of my arm going up, and the causal description of the surroundings: the auction room, and the like. But these are simply further events, to be given further causal descriptions: they cannot introduce reasons to dispute the determinist's analysis of the occurrences of the afternoon, as long as those occurrences are regarded as (bodily) events only; and the two-language view concedes that they can *always* be so regarded. So there is no real choice here, but only an appearance of choice: the bodily movements are inevitable even if the actions are not.

Perhaps the following stylized example helps explain. Imagine a robot that runs on a set of train tracks, the points of which have all been set. The robot approaches a junction in the track and through its brain comes the question, "Shall I turn left or right?" It "decides" to turn right and the track is set up so that, indeed, it does turn that way. The robot might imagine that it had choice, but the choice would be merely an apparent one. Had the robot "decided" to go left, the points were still set for it to go right. The adequacy of the two-language view as a refutation of his or her determinist position can be seriously undermined. It cannot offer more than "choice" (that is, apparent choice) while it remains committed to causal necessity for (bodily) behaviour. The two-language view may help in exploring human explanations of events (in line with p. 90) but nothing, yet, has made us doubt the operation of causal necessity. And, while the movements of bodies are causally necessitated, all talk of action seems unwarranted: choices are at best apparent.

Conclusion

The reasons discussed above (pp. 92–7), and especially the third, give us pause before accepting any two-language, compatibilist or reconciliationist resolution of the problem of free will. Denying the second premise of the determinist argument cannot remove the force of that argument. Even if actions are not a species of movements, actions (and omissions) comprise movements by human bodies: while that is not *all* the story, it is at least part of any story. My buying the table in the auction may not be characterizable solely in movement terms [KEY CASE 10], and my participation in the wedding the Martian watched may be more than just making certain sounds [KEY CASE 9]. Still, the first does involve movements of my arm, and the second sounds coming from my mouth. Once we grant that the movements (including the sound-producing ones) are causally determined, there seems little sense in which these occurrences might *still* be free actions. Those movements are causally necessitated: the free will defence here seems to make action-description somehow superfluous, a kind of "froth" added to what fundamentally happened (which the causal description provides).

To avoid this conclusion, we must take the insights the two-language view offers, but show how this conclusion does not follow (by contesting its account of *causal necessity*, in some situations), while giving due weight to the determinist insight that located causal necessity within scientific explanations. That is the task for the Chapter 8.

The irrelevance
7 **of determinism**

Introduction

Having put aside two of the most usually deployed free will defences, it is worth mentioning two lines of thought that suggest that our problem is misconceived: as such, they might clarify the nature of the determinist challenge. In addition to discharging an obligation to do so (Chapter 3, p. 45), these issues will be considered here because such arguments ground much contemporary discussion of free will related topics: thus a student ignorant of them might find himself or herself at sea in the contemporary literature. As such, they offer research agendas, even if not dealing with our problem. Further, they shed a certain indirect light on the resolution of the problem offered in succeeding chapters.

Since this is the basis for our consideration, these positions can be treated here in broad brush strokes: in neither case need we attend to every detail of every argument, which is especially useful, given the substantial secondary literature.

Both positions challenge the setting-up of the problem of determinism here, by focusing on the relationship between free action and moral responsibility. First (p. 100), arguments derived from Strawson suggest that, since viewing others as moral agents (and seeing ourselves as so viewed) cannot be given up, questions of responsibility cannot depend on resolving those of determinism. So these arguments are pleas for a more realistic understanding of moral responsibility: more importantly, a reconsideration of cases where persons are not treated as responsible. Second (pp. 104–10), arguments derived from Frankfurt challenge the assumed relationship between choice, alternatives and responsibility, by offering cases where, it is urged, there is moral responsibility although the person "could not have done otherwise". In addition to setting useful research agendas, this also prompts reconsideration of the sense in which choice implies that one "could have done otherwise".

"Reactive attitudes"

For Strawson, what must be stressed is:

> the great importance that we attach to the attitudes and intentions towards us of other human beings, and the great extent to which our personal feelings and reactions depend on, or involve, our beliefs about these attitudes and intentions.
>
> (1974: 5)

These Strawson calls "reactive attitudes" (*ibid.*: 6), some of which are "essentially natural human reactions to the good or ill will or indifference of others towards us, as displayed in their attitudes and actions" (*ibid.*: 10), and sometimes explained as "reactions to the quality of others' wills towards us, as manifested in their behaviour: to their good or ill will or indifference or lack of concern" (*ibid.*: 14).

A prime example, enshrined in Strawson's title, is *resentment*: resentment is only justified to the degree to which I have been offended or harmed by the actions of some other persons, in ways I had reason not to expect to be so harmed or offended. Strawson rehearses the variety of excuses potentially deployed to mitigate the action (thereby reducing my resentment), such as "He couldn't help it", or to remove the sense of it as an occasion for resentment: "She was just a child" (with the implication of "therefore morally undeveloped": *ibid.*: 8). Such excuses appeal to the unusual in this case, if effective, they trade off against the usual cases, where such behaviour would justify resentment!

For Strawson, such "reactive attitudes" do not depend for their justification on the falsity of the determinist conclusion. Strawson contrasts such attitudes with the detached position (which he calls "objectivity of attitude") towards the other person that arises when one no longer regards that person's behaviour (and hence that person) as a suitable object of, say, resentment. As Strawson puts it:

> To adopt the objective attitude to another human being is to see him . . . as an object of social policy; as a subject for what . . . might be called treatment . . . The objective attitude . . . cannot include the range of reactive feelings and attitudes.
>
> (*ibid.*: 9)

Thus he begins from "the fact of our natural human commitment to ordinary inter-personal attitudes. This commitment is part of the general framework of human life" (*ibid.*: 13). To proceed on the determinist picture, our lives must be differently conceptualized. But we cannot ourselves make such a move. Such reactive attitudes are too central to our lives (and to our view of them): so we could not (in practice) cease to regard others in ways that presuppose them: "A sustained objectivity of inter-personal attitude, and the isolation which that would entail, does not seem to be something of which human beings would be capable" (*ibid.*: 11). So (Strawson is asserting) humans could not actually behave in these ways. Nor can "failure" to consistently adopt such an "objective" attitude be criticized: "it is useless to ask whether it would not be rational for us to do what it is not in our nature to (be able to) do" (*ibid.*: 18).

Of course, in some cases, such as that of the kleptomaniac [KEY CASE 2], we do adopt such a detached attitude to the behaviour of another. But this case precisely exemplifies Strawson's point: we can do so in this extraordinary case just because we both regard it as extraordinary and because, in not taking the kleptomaniac as a free agent, we thereby remove this person from our usual nexus of reactive attitudes. Such cases will always be the exception, never the rule.

In particular, we could never generally reject ascription of reactive attitudes to others (and to ourselves) on the basis of an abstract argument. So, first: "we cannot, as we are, seriously envisage ourselves adopting a thoroughgoing objectivity of attitude to others as a result of a theoretical conviction of the truth of determinism" (*ibid.*: 12–13). Second: "when we do in fact adopt such an attitude [of objectivity] in a particular case, our doing so . . . is a consequence of our abandoning, for different reasons in different cases, the ordinary inter-personal attitudes" (*ibid.*: 13). So debate on these crucial issues can be conducted independently of the (general) thesis of determinism.

Doing so will require serious attention to the reactive attitudes, in all their variety, seeing their contribution to our moral commitments. For Strawson it is central that: "these practices, and their reception . . . really are expressions of our moral attitudes" (*ibid.*: 25). That is, they are not merely aspects of social engineering, designed to elicit various responses from others: to so regard them detaches from them the moral significance that, for Strawson, is central to these being the practices they are. There is clearly something right in this appeal to a nexus of (normative) rules; an insight from the two-language view. But the determinist under discussion will not countenance mention of such rules (Chapter 6, p. 88), for that assumes what is at issue: the possibility of following such rules (hence of choosing to follow them), as opposed to simply acting in *accordance* with them. Moreover, like the reactive attitudes subtended, these moral commitments are here viewed primarily in terms of the agent's psychology: say, of my moral commitments being reflected in my, for instance, (legitimately) resenting something. But the issue can seem merely psychological: (some of) my apparent decisions will be real decisions only if the reactive attitudes are justified, for only then could my resentment have a basis. But nothing here has addressed the matter of you being an agent in the contested sense: my resenting your action requires that.

As insights, Strawson is stressing the variety of cases that need to be considered in a full treatment. One might think that our "diet of examples" had been quite thin (see Wittgenstein 1953: §593). And the stress on the unusualness or oddity of those cases taken as characteristic of constraint (such as the kleptomaniac [KEY CASE 2]) might be reconsidered (see Chapter 9, p. 142). Moreover, this discussion suggests keeping "the issue of responsibility separate from the issue of free will. Moral responsibility is a moral question" (Thornton 1989: 128).

Equally, though, this position is subject to criticisms (here briefly stated) from the viewpoint of our determinist: first, it defends against psychological determinism, at best – not the most powerful kind, nor that disputed throughout this text. If our commitment to these reactive *attitudes* was a function of, say, various brain-states, humans might inevitably "believe" in such things; that would not make the beliefs true (Wiggins 1987: 299–300). And the determinist is disputing the *truth* of such ascriptions.

Second, the argument appears to be based on some empirical "facts" (better, claims) about how humans do (or could) behave. As we saw, the determinist is unlikely to be much impressed by these. Are Strawson's claims actually true of humans? One might think not.[1] Certainly the variety of ways in which humankind has previously re-thought its relationship with the natural world might give us pause here: can we really be as certain as Strawson is? Our determinist will urge that we *cannot*, offering as a counter-case the one person who can consistently adopt to fellow beings the "objectivity of attitude" needed; again, this cannot be guaranteed to be impossible.

Against this line, Strawson's position is that reactive attitudes provide background constraints for the very possibility of experience: thus, this is not the empirical argument it seems. But, now, more needs to be said in defence of the argument-form (contrast Trusted 1984: 143–4), and of its ascription to Strawson. At the least, it is not obvious how this line of argument could be elaborated.

A third difficulty involves the suggestion that, far from showing the irrelevance of determinism to issues of responsibility, Strawson simply *assumes* a free will defence. Strawson's issue is: "whether it would not be rational, given a general theoretical conviction of the truth of determinism, so to change our world that in it all these [reactive] attitudes were suspended" (Strawson 1974: 18). But this suggests that our attitudes are amenable to change: that we might decide or choose to do so, precisely what our determinist denies. For these would be actions as much as any other. And personal reports of choosing cannot be just accepted. The kleptomaniac [KEY CASE 2] might claim to have chosen, say, to take the scarf from the department store (Chapter 1, p. 4), but the kleptomaniac's behaviour was not, in the relevant sense, action at all. To repeat that point: the conception of human life as centrally involving choice is precisely the one that the determinist denies, a denial rooted in his or her argument (Chapter 2, p. 21). Faced with this argument, it will not do simply to re-assert the possibility of action. The determinist recognizes that his or her argument would undercut much, perhaps all, of how we think of ourselves. But that is precisely the point: a determinist may even give up such notions as rationality. The determinist will urge the *truth* of his or her position, no matter how it conflicts with standard views of ourselves (compare Wiggins 1987: 299–300), even if (psychologically) we cannot give up this view.

So this is not a way of meeting our determinist argument: its attempt to separate reactive attitudes (and hence morality) from questions of determinism fails if considered simply as a claim about what humans will continue to believe (which is irrelevant) and it cannot establish the priority of such issues.[2]

Morality and variety of outcomes

The other argument also turn on the relationship of free will to morality, especially moral responsibility. Its focus is the assumed connection between *responsibility* and *alternatives*: that I can be responsible only if I "could have done otherwise" than I did. Here, Frankfurt's position amounts to an explanation-via-example of his general thesis that an agent might be responsible despite no alternative action being open to him or her.

These examples (sometimes called "Frankfurt-type examples": Fischer 1994: 131;[3] Kane 1996: 40–43) work in the following way. Suppose Green wants Grey to perform some particular action; say, to vote for the Conservative party in the up-coming election. If Grey simply decides to vote Conservative, Green need do nothing. But should Grey not so decide, Green has a fall-back position. In his capacity as Grey's neurosurgeon, he has implanted a microchip in Grey's brain: once it becomes clear to him how Grey means to vote (and Green "is an excellent judge of such things" (Frankfurt 1969: 835)), Green will activate the device, thereby causing Grey to vote Conservative. So either Grey decides to vote Conservative, which coincides with Green's plan, and Green does nothing, or (second case) Grey would have voted for some other party had not Green, getting wind of this, activated the device: now Grey again "votes" Conservative. So only one outcome is possible. Under the first possibility, Grey *does* choose (it seems) and is responsible for his action (his share of the blame for the dreadful policies the Conservatives then implement, etc.). Our conviction that he chooses is rooted in the fact that, as van Inwagen puts it, "the causal history of his act [in this case] is just what it would have been if [Green] had never existed" (1983: 163). But he could not do otherwise. So this seems a case of moral responsibility despite only one outcome being possible. Such examples illustrate how an agent might be responsible even though no alternative action is open to him or her.[4]

Any contrary emphasis is clearly on freedom of the will, which Frankfurt explicitly contrasts with the freedom of action: this discussion concerns what constitutes freely *willing* – and that contrasts with our emphasis (throughout this text) on freely *acting*, since the problem under discussion concerned the possibility of (genuine) action.

Some implications of Frankfurt-type cases

If choice implies alternatives, then lack of alternatives may preclude choice, and hence responsibility, and that is the determinist conclusion. The relationship of free will to responsibility was taken (Chapter 1, p. 5) to follow from this: that one could only be responsible for what one had chosen to do. Now, Frankfurt-type cases affect only this inference: at best, they show that one might have responsibility without choice. (Were this true, determinism might fail to *absolutely* preclude responsibility, even if it absolutely precluded choice, by concluding that the notion of choice had no (genuine) application.)

What is the upshot of the Frankfurt-type cases? As van Inwagen points out, such cases do not imply: "that we might be morally responsible for our acts even if we lacked free will; it follows only that the usual argument for the proposition that moral responsibility entails free will has a false premise" (van Inwagen 1983: 164). One might simply conclude that such cases remove an argument for relating freedom to (moral) responsibility, without giving us reason to actually doubt that relationship. Here, though, the aim is to see what such Frankfurt-type cases show about the connection of choice to alternatives.

Notice that Frankfurt-type cases are not symmetrical: if Grey acts without Green's intervention, we have no difficulty in regarding him as a free agent (although this is the common-sense position, or free will defender's, not the determinist's). Yet is this action free? There can only be one outcome: Grey can only choose one way; and the interesting case is the one where Grey makes that choice (as it were) *independently*. In the second scenario, once Green has acted, Grey is not choosing at all. (We might even doubt that this behaviour was a genuine action.)

Now consider other cases of apparent (but not real) choice. One cannot choose to do what is physically impossible: one cannot, for example, choose to jump over the moon (Chapter 1, p. 7); at best, one might (foolishly) aspire to do so. Yet, subjectively, one thinks one was so choosing. This conclusion resembles that from Frankfurt-type cases: that I "choose", where such "choice" is treated in terms of my (internal) psychology, does not prove that I am free. Equally, if there are only cheese salads in the cafeteria, my renowned fondness for cheese salad might justify my claim that I chose a cheese salad: in different circumstances, I would have chosen a cheese salad. But there was no choice – or, better, no real choice among salads (see Chapter 6, p. 93). This, too, resembles the conclusion from the Frankfurt-type case; the feeling of having chosen does not guarantee that one chose, in a world where (some?) choice is only apparent.

With only cheese salads in the cafeteria, there was no choice for dinner. So one could not choose; at least, one could not choose, say, a ham salad. This case resembles both the attempt to select a physically impossible course of action, and also a Frankfurt-type case. In an apt expression of Nathan (1992: 111), here the "freedom of field" is lacking. To better understand one aspect of such cases, consider a scenario in which, say, I decide (in advance) on the cheese salad, expecting there to be a choice; or one in which the options are concealed from me – it is a salad lucky-dip. Now, I have chosen, in the sense of deciding, even though there is in actuality no choice. Here I might be judged (praised, blamed and the like) for, roughly, the *decision* without regard to whether any action followed. And, as a salad-selector, the notion of choice applies to me in general, even if its application to the case under consideration is less clear. There was no real choice, but I am a real chooser. (And, notice, this is of a piece with Frankfurt's decision (noted above: p. 104) to discuss the issue from the "agent's" viewpoint.) So one part of the inclination to regard Grey as responsible, in the first option of the Frankfurt-type case, is that here he decided to vote Conservative: indeed, he might be held responsible even where the election was cancelled at the last minute.

So did Grey really choose in the scenario where Green does not (have to) intervene? Perhaps not. Equally, perhaps the case rests on Grey's responsibility for what he *would have* chosen, had there been a choice. Here the case of the absent ham salad above seems closer to real choice than the case of Grey. For the chooser is not "impaired" by the absence of the ham salad: by contrast, Grey either chooses in line with Green's desires, or he does not get to choose at all.

So there are two distinct senses in which "there was no choice". In the first, I am a chooser but the expected options are not available (whether or not I know this). There is no choice, because there are only cheese salads in the lucky-dip cafeteria. It seems right here to look to my intentions, my plans, my desires and the like: if there is praise or blame "in the offing", this is how to best distribute it. In the second case, no choice is available to me because Green-type intervention precludes me from being a chooser at all: the notion of choice does not apply to me. There is no choice because there could be no choosing, even at the level of selecting between decisions, or intentions: we can imagine Green's device controls these too.

Were this right, it displays the structure of the Frankfurt-type case, as I have described it. The two options combine the two senses of "there was no choice": either Grey is a chooser, but the voting "salad-bar" has only Conservatives, or he is not. Rather, he is *compelled* to behave as he does (and even this description puts the matter too close to agency).

Consider two of the ways in which one "could not help" what occurred: in the following case (which I quote both for the charming language and the charming view of university life that it contains):

> a Russian guest at dinner in my college inadvertently sprinkles a lot of salt on his or her pudding, mistaking it for sugar, and so renders his or her pudding unpalatable; and suppose that for some reason I am reproached for this *contretemps*, and am told that I ought to have prevented it.
>
> (Warnock in Pears 1963: 71, original emphasis)

Two common-sense contrasts are appropriate here. First, I could not have prevented the Russian doing as he did since I was both seated too far from him to have intervened, and unable to speak Russian. So (roughly) both one's location (facts external to one) and one's abilities are relevant to what one can do. Second, my colleague Jenkins could have prevented the Russian doing this; she was close enough and Russian-speaking. So my inability to do the thing is contrasted with another's ability. Both of these are within the realm of human agency, of course: they indicate, respectively, ways to justify the claim "I could not help it", and an implication from the fact that I could not help it, namely, that another could. Importantly, in this case, factors external to me are relevant to what I could or could not (choose to) do, a point worth expanding.

Consider a parallel here. Imagine a transporter device, as used in *Star Trek*, such that a person may be transported from a spaceship to the planet's surface. One day, the machine malfunctions, and two Captain Kirks arrive on the planet's surface: which is the real Captain Kirk? Our concepts of identity and difference are not equipped to deal with such hypothetical cases. Since both have equal claim, neither can be regarded as Captain Kirk: *one* is, as it were, the only suitable answer here. And such a conclusion might be reinforced by reflecting on the way that neither of the successor-amoebae is the very same one as the parent: again, they cannot both be, and there is no reason to prefer one over the other; *one* is the only suitable answer.

Whatever one makes of this case itself, it illustrates two points: we must not assume that our concepts can readily deal with all cases; and facts about the external surroundings (of one of the Captain Kirks) might have a bearing on the appropriate description. Similarly, we might conclude that Grey was responsible in the case where he decides to vote Conservative and Green does nothing. If we so conclude, it is because we recognize his intention here, regarding him as a chooser. We treat him as though he stated immediately before entering the cafeteria that he would choose a cheese salad; and did so. The absence of ham salad (or any other alternative) was irrelevant. Equally, the fact that Green will intervene if Grey comes to any other choice has a bearing. It modifies his situation, even though it does not directly affect Grey himself (affect the molecules of his body, as it were). Yet there is no choice in this case, just as one is bound to end up with cheese salad if one lunches in that cafeteria! Both these intuitions seem right. Notice, first, that if we do regard Grey as responsible in this case, it is because we regard him as a chooser, and, to that degree, as free. If, instead, we emphasize that there was no choice, we will not attribute special praise or blame here. Second, the facts of the case are clear. If we remain unclear what to do or say, that may well be because these concepts are unresolved for such hypothetical examples.

To elaborate a response to a Frankfurt-type example, reconsider Strawson's position (p. 100): Green's neurosurgical activities, whether they result in an intervention or not, make this an odd or unusual case, one where we have (in that fact) a justification for modifying our attitude to Grey's behaviour (and to Grey). Of course, in practice, such a case might easily go unnoticed: Grey is easily mistaken for a free agent even if Green has intervened, and even more straightforwardly, perhaps, if he has not. But our (practical) mistake would not alter the logic of the case; it is agreed on all sides that Grey is not a free agent in the scenario where Green intervenes, and so our mistakes are neither here nor there. Rather, they are indeed mistakes.

One dimension of the asymmetry (mentioned earlier) between the Frankfurt-type options is to reject the suggestion that Green's intervention leaves Grey's choices unaffected (because there is no causal intervention). A second dimension reflects the fact that, contrary to Frankfurt's assertion, the outcomes of the two scenarios are not equivalent. In one, Grey is an agent, so an action is performed; in the other, there is no agency (unless it is Green's agency). Here, a precise account of the outcome – of what occurred – in each of the scenarios must reflect this difference.

What does this tell us about the demand that free agents "could have done otherwise"? Frankfurt-type cases show that this alone is not a sufficiently detailed characteriszation of free action (Locke 1975): it can be defeated in ways that preserve responsibility (or seem to). Grey could not do otherwise than he did but, if Frankfurt is right, he is responsible (or plausibly taken to be so). Yet this is achieved, in the case where he does as he wished (say, votes Conservative), exactly as it would be if his other choices had not been "interfered with" by Green. That tempts us to think he must be responsible here: this would be a free action, if only . . . What precludes Grey doing otherwise is another's agency, not the working out of causal laws. So this case attributes agency *both* to the original agent (Grey) and to the one who wants to make the outcome inevitable (Green). In such a case, Grey "could not have done otherwise" for reasons that cite either his agency or the agency of another. This case should not interest a determinist much: he should dispute *these* elements of agency, as others.

Here, the reason why the agent "could not have done otherwise" might be relevant: and this highlights that the nature of the determinism under discussion is itself a crucial topic for consideration (Chapter 2, p. 28). Here, physical causality has provided the determining "explanations" throughout, a fact that has coloured the "forces" that have been taken throughout to preclude "doing otherwise" than one actually does. Thus a crucial insight from these considerations (from Frankfurt) has in fact played a part throughout this text.

Conclusion

In considering two ways of avoiding some implications of the determinist challenge, this chapter has shown that, however insightful, these two strategies fail to defuse determinism. First, neither aims to refute the determinist. As Wiggins (1987: 300) notes, Strawson's position is not a compatibilist one; while Frankfurt disputes a supposed conclusion (in fact, a supposed argument) linking choice and responsibility. Second, both are concerned with freedom in *willing*, whereas our determinist disputed the possibility of genuine action (not just feeling free). If one might criticize Strawson's argumentative strategy for staying too close to the empirical/practical, the opposite might be urged against Frankfurt: we are asked to consider cases well beyond likelihood, with no guarantee that the concepts invoked will have application in these novel situations. But both emphasize the complexity of cases where action and responsibility are ascribed to human behaviour; and both recognize that the cases that fuel this discussion are somehow unusual, typically contrasted with a "usual" background of human agency.

The very idea of
8 causal necessity

Introduction – the problem outlined

In addressing my own view of an appropriate free will defence, I offer something both slightly more technical and certainly more speculative than elsewhere. The technicality is warranted both because, this late in the text, readers are ready for it and because it offers hope for a solution.

As we have seen, there is no mileage in objecting to premise 1 of the determinist argument; further, while the two-language view may oblige the determinist to make some drafting changes (Chapter 6, p. 95), the force of premise 2 of the determinist argument cannot be avoided in that two-language way: the notion of choice is undermined. None the less, the two-language view offers some insights, in emphasizing the importance of context; seeing answers as understood in terms of the question being asked, rather than in some neutral way. Although we cannot appeal in the same way to the importance of context for causal explanation, perhaps something may be learned about causation from this characterization. As we saw earlier (also McFee 1992: 63–4), causal explanations too might operate in response to specific questions. For instance, requests to know the length of some object might admit different answers when different issues were assumed (also Chapter 8, p. 122).

So the "insight" of the two-language view was (roughly) that actions are not causally necessitated because action-description is context-sensitive. This did not defeat determinism: since causes *did* necessitate in the destructive sense, the bodily movements

...ng any actions (or omissions) were necessitated, even if the ...ns were not (Chapter 6, p. 95–6). So the two-language view combated determinism too much in its own terms, only contesting its view of action. It granted that determinist conclusions were warranted, as long as he or she confined attention to causal explanation. In contrast, I shall suggest that the determinist was wrong about causal explanation (too). Equally, the moral from Chapter 4, one does not contest the *analysis* of causality by denying causality as such.

Twentieth-century images of causation can have no direct impact, although this point is often misunderstood (see Appendix). As Chapter 4 showed us, no discussion couched exclusively in terms of science could ever meet the challenge of the determinist argument: first, the determinist builds on ideas central to the project of science; in particular, the possibility of causal explanation, without remainder, of the world around us. As our consideration of the Bermuda Triangle showed (Chapter 2, p. 23), this powerful assumption is shared on all sides. Second, a free will defence essentially defends the possibility of agency: that is, it defends the contrast between agency and events explained causally. Such a distinction cannot be drawn solely within the province of the causal. Yet a revised image of science cannot offer anything else here; as science, those images would not distinguish action from happening, but rather necessarily apply to both.

My argument begins by identifying two assumptions implicit in the conception of causes as necessitating, both originating in the determinist view of causes as "antecedent states of the world" (Chapter 2, p. 21). First, where A is the cause of B, there is a "finite totality of possibilities" to consider, a number of situations any of which (if they occurred) would defuse the implication that B is *bound* to occur, given the occurrence of A. In principle, this catalogue of possibilities might all be considered (a finite totality of counter-possibilities). Second, causal descriptions of various parts or aspects of the world might, in principle, be conjoined. So, for example, true descriptions of the motion both of the planet Jupiter and of its moons could be combined, with enough ingenuity, into a description of the motion of the planet Jupiter and its moons. Although this assumption has a certain plausibility for the natural sciences, it has little plausibility applied to descriptions of actions, where different contexts (or different issues) generate different descriptions of events: this is a major insight of the two-language view, which disputed the second of the determinist assumptions, at least as applied to action. (We saw, in Chapter 6, that this defence cannot withstand the determined determinist.) Yet my thesis is, first, that, on investigation, neither of the two determinist assumptions identified can be sustained and, second, that this is sufficient to refute the determinist argument.

Of course, free will defences must ensure that they indeed generate free will. My response (expanded in Chapter 9) has two dimensions. First, the essential challenge to free will is provided via the determinist argument (Chapter 2). Thus, to conclude (in a principled way) that the determinist conclusion does not follow from that argument *is* to have established free will: no reason remains *not* to accept the freedom of the will (once we recognize that the real issue is "Are there actions?" rather than "Are actions free?"). Second, I show why the problem arises: why a committed thinker on these (metaphysical?) topics might take seriously the determinist challenge. Too simple a way of dealing with the issue leaves mysterious its enduring "appeal": we must acknowledge the explanatory role of causality.

Causes do necessitate, at least in natural science, and the determinist (rightly) has repeatedly referred to this commitment of natural science. We can now explain (p. 127) why it is a commitment (by seeing that it is exactly that!). So the slogan "Every event has a cause" (the first premise in our determinist argument) means that, if one looks at an occurrence as an event, there will be a causal story . . . nothing escapes science in this sense. And, in answering questions in science, causes are seen as necessitating.

The net outcome is that we provide the inexorability of causal laws, by not permitting "deviation". Perhaps this is wrong of the natural world (although how could we know?) but we do – and must (for the project of science) – assume it. Yet we don't need to assume it for actions.

Causal necessity – a determinist's view

The two determinist assumptions (identified above) are both visible in the use, sometimes implicit, that the determinist argument makes of the idea of other things being equal: as we shall say, of *ceteris paribus* clauses. How might that point be made explicit?

According to the determinist view, there is some ultimate description of events – although, of course, we typically do not, and perhaps cannot, know this description. The determinist thinks his or her question is, "What is really going on?" – as it were, absolutely, fundamentally; and therefore the true reply, if it could be got (Bradley 1969 [1893]: 506), would be an "absolute conception of the world" (Williams 1985: 139); that is, a set of mutually consistent, true, conjoined descriptions of the workings of the world. For the determinist, this is in the project of twentieth-century science: describing the workings of the world, without remainder. Of course, particular descriptions will typically be incomplete, failing to specify all the details needed for causal necessity. Perhaps they must be incomplete, given the variety and complexity of factors to be considered even in so simple a case as the interaction of billiard balls [KEY CASE 8]. For any predictions here could be vitiated not only by "local" conditions (dust on the table, chalk on one of the balls) but also by more distant factors (the gravitational effect of the arrival of comets, or of changes at the galactic centre). Here, recognizing this plurality of conditions as relevant concedes something about their mutual combinability. In practice, these possibilities are handled via *ceteris paribus* clauses: very roughly, when things did not turn out as predicted, it is because "other things" were not equal (in specifiable ways).

Determinist argumentation is built on the idea that causes *necessitate* (if *A* is the cause of *B* then, if *A* occurs, *B* (and only *B*) is bound to occur) – of course, only *ceteris paribus*. As we have seen in our billiards example [KEY CASE 8], for different outcomes, there must be some differences in initial conditions, say, although we cannot (yet?) specify in what ways they differ: "there must be a difference between the first and the second situations, or there would have been the same outcome". So there is an assumed background to those things we might actually check (was there chalk on the cue-ball, for instance?). Such a background represents those "things that must be equal", often put as a *ceteris paribus* clause, which are taken for granted. So causes are necessitating only once the background is filled in: that is, the *ceteris paribus* clause spelled out. This means spelling out how things are, in contrast to how they might have been, paying special attention to those possibilities that might "upset the apple cart". In seeing causes as necessitating, the determinist assumes that such spelling-out can always be done (at least in principle): that is, he or she assumes that there is a finite totality of such possibilities for, without this being so, *all* the possibilities could not be spelled-out; there would be no "all possibilities".

Notice, though, the move here from hesitations we might *have* (and might check – it is sensible to consider chalk on the cue-ball) via considerations that might be raised (if we know of passing comets, perhaps a check on their gravitational effects is warranted) to an unspecifiable *anything* that might go wrong so as to upset our prediction. (Our criticism begins from here.)

So, the determinist's use of (implicit?) *ceteris paribus* clauses implies a finite totality of (counter-) possibilities, a finite number of "things" to be equal, or of ways in which things might "go wrong": that is, all the factors that might result in some outcome other than *B*, in the presence of *A*, and in a situation where *A* is the cause of *B* (our example concerned the interaction between billiard balls: KEY CASE 8). In modelling causation in this way, the determinist acts as though, in principle, one could "fill in" the list of "things being equal": to do so would import the assumption of a finite totality of possibilities.

Further, *ceteris paribus* clauses focus our attention on one element of the causal chain, so that other elements will be absorbed as the "other things being equal", as though true causal descriptions or causal "stories" could always be conjoined. This is indeed implicit in the key idea of a *causal chain* (Chapter 1, p. 6): *A* caused *B*, and *B* caused *C*: therefore (at one remove) *A* caused *C*. So, a (true or correct) causal account of *one* event can always be conjoined with a (true or correct) causal account of another event, with the result being true. Thus, a complete causal account of the universe (etc.) at any moment could, in principle, be constructed. And, even if we actually lack such accounts, that is merely a practical limitation, a limitation on human knowledge (perhaps, reflecting the present state of human knowledge). For commitment to the first premise of the determinist argument grants that there always are causal stories, whether humans know them or not. This commitment to conjoinable causal stories will give an "absolute conception of the world", a thought essential to the determinist since the cause referred to (in premise 4: Chapter 2, p. 21) is indeed an antecedent state of the world.

Both of the determinist's assumptions flow from his or her treatment of *ceteris paribus* clauses. If either assumption is given up, the determinist must give up his or her use of *ceteris paribus* clauses: but then he or she cannot write causal laws, at least, not ones that necessitate. For, with no *ceteris paribus* clause, A may cause B (for instance, the billiard balls of KEY CASE 8) on one occasion while, on another occasion, A can occur and B not occur; the situation being one otherwise picked up by a *ceteris paribus* clause, and where, because something different occurred, the initial conditions must have been different. So giving up *ceteris paribus* permits inexplicable happenings or failings to happen, whereas the essence of causal necessity was that, if A occurred and A caused B, then B (and only B) was bound to occur.

Yet, with causes not necessitating in that way, there is no move from the thesis of universal causation (determinist premise 1), even for bodily movements (Chapter 6, p. 95), to the denial of either the possibility of choice, or of the cogency of the "language" of action (determinist conclusions). For only causal necessity means that, in just that situation, just one outcome is possible. (And that is the substance of determinist premise 4: Chapter 2, p. 21.)

One difficulty now concerns the idea of "just that situation": there is no finite totality of characteristics to be considered to make it "just that situation' (and no other), hence no way of deciding what we can know, decide or consider. For there is no "just that situation", because there is no precise sets of ways (no finite totality of possibilities) in which it differs from other situations.

So the strategy of this chapter, therefore, is to argue that, since the determinist's assumptions are not generally sustainable, the determinist argument can be rejected. Earlier (Chapter 2, p. 24), a practical objection to determinism was considered: that a "*combinatorial explosion*" (Dennett 1991: 5) would preclude the acquiring of knowledge of causal processes and hence of initial conditions. This strategy effectively turns that practical objection into a theoretical one: it is not that we cannot (as a matter of fact) do X, but that the expression "doing X" makes no sense because, for it to do so, the explanation must embrace a finite number of factors (there must be a finite totality of possibilities, where correct accounts are conjoinable), and this is not so.

Now can we argue that either or both of the determinist's assumptions should be given up? In what follows, I shall urge that both are implausible.

The search for counter-possibilities

To review our situation: we accept premise 1 of the determinist argument, and acknowledge that the force of premise 2 cannot be avoided; even if actions were not a species of event, the bodily movements comprising them were (Chapter 6, p. 96). We will be assailing premise 4, to suggest that the notion of causation does not necessarily bring with it causal necessity; and thus evade the determinist conclusion.

Suppose I assert that, once a particular car's handbrake is released, it will inevitably run into the wall situated downhill from it [KEY CASE 14].[1] In doing so, I presuppose that the natural world is operating "normally": for me, "normally" here does not include the possibility of an earthquake – after all, this is no earthquake zone. (If I were just unfamiliar with the area, and did not think to consider the possibility of earthquakes, my failure might be ignorance: that is not the case under consideration.) You deny that this car will indeed hit the wall on the grounds that there might be an earthquake. Now, first, you must look more widely than the causal interaction of car, wall and road, and even that is part of a causal chain stretching back indefinitely. Second, you must make the suggestion of an earthquake plausible: the mere possibility of earthquakes on the earth is not sufficient (so the burden of providing a reason for the investigation is yours). Third, this suggestion invites me to investigate *only* the possibility of there being an earthquake.

But this is not how you proceed. Instead, when I have ruled out that possibility, you raise another such possibility, and so forth. Each seems a possibility to be ruled out in order to (fully) justify my initial assertion. That is to say, in order to set up the initial conditions so that my causal law, in this case the law of gravity, is operative, it *seems* that all these possibilities must be ruled out. If I accept your way of proceeding, I am granting both a role for the ruling-out of counter-possibilities and the conception that some possibilities should be considered, in principle.

Notice, though, a more reasonable set of responses here: I did not need to check for earthquakes, There has never been one in this part of the world, theory gives us no reason to expect one now, and there are no other "signs" (etc.) that should induce investigation of this "possibility". In particular, the mere insistence that it *is* a possibility does not supply a reason. Rather, the burden of proof is on the person who requires the additional checks be carried out; additional, that is, to those required by theory, local knowledge and other "conventionally presupposed constancies" (Hampshire 1989: 87). Given your alarmism, perhaps I now have a reason to go beyond these precautions in just this respect: but then, greeted with yet more of your dire "possibilities", I will be right to ignore them. There is no finite totality of checks to make, or of (possibly) relevant considerations. I cannot (even in principle) demonstrate that all other things are equal, since there is no finite totality of "other things". So the determinist hope smoothly to employ a *ceteris paribus* clause to provide the background to allow causes genuinely to necessitate is misplaced.

What is really there?[2]

Now, turn to the second determinist assumption: the possibility of conjoining descriptions. A second aspect of our consideration, for the next section, explores the very idea of such a determinate number of possibilities, by asking how such descriptions might "fit together" (or conjoin): in particular, whether they *necessarily* can do so. The first aspect, broached in this section, asks if causal descriptions have context-sensitivity: for, if they have, only descriptions from the same (or, perhaps, similar) contexts could be conjoined.

The determinist urges that there is, as it were, a primary description of all occurrences, including those involving human beings: the description given by science (Chapter 6, p. 92). But is there one consistent description offered by science? Can different aspects be accommodated smoothly into one global or comprehensive description? There is no reason to suppose that this is true. Having once accepted the reality of actions (Chapter 6, p. 91), we have identified aspects of the world that, while not escaping scientific scrutiny, are none the less ill-served when described or explained solely causally.

Notice, too, that the question "what is really there?" could be answered by giving any of a number of descriptions, even if we consider only causal descriptions: the description "collection of elementary particles in such-and-such configurations" is not always preferable to the description "human being", or "homo sapiens". The word "really" in the question seemed to imply that the answer required offers a deeper or more profound account of "reality". But it cannot do this. For the descriptions given are not necessarily compatible.

Consider, for example, describing a table as a collection of (point) atoms with large spaces between them:[3] for some purposes, this is a true description of the table. Equally, seeing the table as solid object is also true of it, but from a different perspective. Different questions are being addressed, but both are causal questions. Those of us concerned about, say, the table's ability to support glasses of beer are not centrally interested in its molecular structure: crucial to us is precisely that it is a continuous surface not a collection of spaced objects, even if we grant that this is achieved via its molecular composition. We would resist any effort to claim that the other view was true, or, rather, we would (correctly) not see this answer as addressing our issue or concern. Must such descriptions be conjoinable? No: both descriptions are true but nothing (other than a prior commitment) guarantees that they will fit together. After all, the purposes do not (necessarily) fit together. In this sense, causal description is as point-of-view dependent, or context-dependent, as action-description.

For instance, the contrast between custom-cars and hot-rods designates production models modified for "look" and speed respectively. Describing a custom-car's properties, we may neglect to mention that it has an engine. Indeed, imagine an extreme custom-car where the polished "cylinder" block was simply decorative. Equally, an extreme hot-rod might be profoundly unaesthetic. At the least, recognizing (of some non-extreme version) what makes such-and-such a custom-car – or, indeed, a good custom-car – might plausibly not mention just those features central to a vehicle's being a hot-rod: such features would be "custom-car-irrelevant" features. Mentioning them in a discussion of custom-cars would illustrate ignorance, misunderstanding or some such. Yet one and the same car might be a hot-rod (on Tuesday) and a custom-car (on Wednesday): as it were, it might be presented to two audiences. What are the car's real features? Emphasizing its line, say, will not be recognizing its aerodynamic characteristics: why should we assume both could necessarily be parts of one (conjoined) description? Here, each concern (each description) satisfies its question, but there is no overall or conjoined description.[4]

Where does this leave the determinist assumption that true descriptions can *always* be conjoined? When those descriptions serve radically different purposes, there is no reason to suppose that they can be conjoined without remainder. But this clarifies the insight the determinist exploits: in some cases, such conjoining will typically be possible, with cases from natural science being prime candidates. The determinist argument mistakenly assumes this as the general situation: that we could always conjoin, or that there is an ultimate (true) description. Descriptions at the same "level" can be "conjoined"; that is, when the same question is being addressed, or when the same background assumptions are made (the same *ceteris paribus* invoked). Although applying to actions as to events, this may be more regularly used in respect of events (for instance, in descriptions by "hard science").

Confusingly, the very same sentence, the same form of words, can amount to many different questions, or to the raising of different issues (see the drunken husband's misunderstanding, Chapter 6, p. 90; and Chapter 8, p. 123). So we cannot assume, finding the same string of words, that the *same* issue is always being addressed (Travis 1989: 18–19). For example, identifying which point is raised (in context) by the claim that Raku is a city of half a million (Travis 1981: 148–51) can suggest, say, different ways of disputing it: Raku has fewer than half a million people, although the "feel" is of a city that size; or its present size (over half a million) warrants more government support; or its population is actually half a million and one (and thus the claim is false). And so on. Thus the sameness of words alone cannot guarantee sameness of issue.

The inexhaustibility of description

Turning to the practicalities of describing a certain event, even a causal description "picks out salient relationships between salient features from the inexhaustible network of actual features in reality" (Hampshire 1989: 87). That is, a typical explanation of causal relations will not in practice involve ruling out all counter-possibilities but rather will invoke a clause to the effect that other things are equal (a *ceteris paribus* clause), assuming the uniformity or constancy of background within which the precise causal law is taken to operate.[5] Otherwise, exceptions might occur. In seeing causes as *always* necessitating, the determinist assumes that this could always be done, at least in principle.

To avoid the conclusion that, since the *ceteris paribus* clauses could never be fully spelled out, causes did *not* necessitate, the determinist insists that the practicalities of prediction are not the issue. Since free will defenders agree, our attention is on the assumption that moves the determinist from the actuality of our inability to predict to the predictability in principle; the assumption of a determinate world "out there", a finite totality of possibilities. For (as we have seen), with no such finite totality, the idea of checking *all* the possibilities makes no sense: the word "all" would lack meaning in that context.

Now, however many details of the situation are specified, still others, if actualized, would turn it from a case where event *X* will happen to one where *X* might not, or even will not happen. The causal laws, applied in these conditions, lead to this outcome. But, for instance, what initial conditions must be specified to "fill in" the inexorability of the car's running down the hill and into the wall [KEY CASE 14]? This is just the point about a "finite totality of possibilities" writ small. If our description of those initial conditions fails to mention a rock big enough to divert the downhill passage of the car, the required inexorability will not be arrived at. For that rock's presence explains why something else (other than the predicted) occurs. So any rock of sufficient size to induce deviation in the car's path requires mention, as does any depression in the ground that has the same effect; but then so does any relevant meteorite that might destroy the car, or any comet, the gravitational effects of which might have a bearing. Our only way of picking out what to consider is by speaking of its *relevance*: yet that is precisely what cannot be known in advance of consideration of the possible effects. We are returning to the realm of "all counter-possibilities", as though there were a finite totality – although now applied to particular cases. This list of (potentially) relevant factors is indefinitely long, with the only summary being to say that *relevant* considerations must be noted. But this just highlights the sense in which description here is inevitably "inexhaustible" (Hampshire 1982 [1959]: 21, 1989: 88): that one cannot specify – in the abstract, and in advance of investigation – a set of factors that will *always* be the relevant ones in *all* cases.

This example employs a causal story, with no hint of agency in the elements under consideration. So that finding ourselves unable to specify the relevant conditions speaks to our more general difficulties with characterizing the antecedent state of the world, as required for premise 4 of the determinist argument. Hampshire's way of expressing this point might be misunderstood: the thought behind "the inexhaustibility of description" is not that the description is really incomplete, such that (in principle) it could be completed (Baker & Hacker 1980: 79). Rather, no description closes off *all* avenues of elaboration: if we took the description as essentially incomplete, it would be because, by some model of completeness (on which all questions are answered), there is always more to be said. But this "more" is a way of rejecting just that model of completeness.

Yet this is the very model of completeness, of covering all cases (if only via a *ceteris paribus* clause), that the determinist uses to account for that combination of "causal-law-plus-specified-initial conditions" that renders the later state of affairs (the effect) inevitable, by causal necessity. But the initial conditions cannot be specified so as to address all factors relevant to the causal implications of those conditions, for there is no all here, no finite totality of conditions.

How is such "inexhaustibility" explained? Asked the length of a particular table [KEY CASE 15] (see McFee 1992: 64), an appropriate answer will depend on precisely what is being asked, on the context of the question, for if that question addresses the need to get the table through a doorway, giving an answer to six decimal places will not be an example of precision but of silly overkill. On the other hand, six decimal places may be just what is needed if the question about the table is to function in testing in the accuracy of my new micrometer. In this way, the causal explanation too has a sensitivity to context, to that degree. So one way to explain the "inexhaustibility of description" is by reference to (what I shall call[6]) the *speaking variability* of causal utterances, that they too should be seen as answers to precise questions, and cannot therefore be treated as neutral. Each of the questions that might be asked using a particular form of words represents a (not necessarily compatible) description, picking out a different possibility. So one explanation here might lie in a quite general feature of understanding; in recognizing *speaking variability* or accepting the *speaking-sensitive* view of words (Travis 1991: 242).

So there is not one, fundamental description of what occurs that science, for example, could present us with. Asked about the size of the table, our answer was related to the purpose of the enquiry: there was no ultimate answer, because there was no ultimate question. But the determinist thinks he or she is asking what is really, fundamentally, going on. That (as we have seen) is the first of his or her errors.

Further, the determinist presents *ceteris paribus* clauses as though they were simply a shorthand for a set of details that we could, in principle, fill in, had we but world enough and time! But descriptions of those details are inexhaustible, because of the variety of concerns. So the determinist assumption of fully or completely expressed *ceteris paribus* clauses for causal interactions is a vain hope.

Yet causes do have a role here in all cases: nothing escapes science by entering an enclave of the counter-causal (as Campbell claimed: Chapter 4, p. 54), nor does science itself yield the counter-causal (in line with the pretensions of the uncertainty principle: Chapter 4, p. 60). Every event has a causal story, so this is not libertarianism. My strategy recognizes causal descriptions and explanations as context-responsive, although not in quite the same way as action-descriptions and explanations.

Defeasibility

To better understand the operation of the "inexhaustibility of description", we shall introduce a technical notion: that of *defeasibility* (McFee 1992: 61ff.). The model for defeasibility comes from the law, where the notion *contract* is defeasible. This means that, once certain conditions are satisfied, there is a contract between us. But there so being a contract may be defeated if someone denying the contract can prove that a recognized "heads of exception" is satisfied. Although the "heads of exception" are normally expressed as a positive-sounding condition (that the contract be "true, full and free"), this is just shorthand for various kinds of objection that someone who denied that there was a contract might raise, having accepted that the major conditions for there being a contract were satisfied. For defeasible notions, the burden of proof is on the objector, once the initial conditions are satisfied. That is to say, given that these conditions are satisfied, there is a contract between us: if you wish to deny that, it is up to you as objector to consider defeating "possibilities". So any "counter-possibilities" are to be considered only in so far as they apply in *this* case, rather than simply as abstract possibilities. Further, we did not know precisely what things were required to be equal when we imagined that all counter-possibilities must be ruled out. In contrast, in wishing to object to a contract (or the application of any other defeasible notion), I know fairly precisely what considerations are relevant, for they are the considerations picked up by the "heads of exception" (Baker 1977: 52–3).

Hampshire (1989: 14) remarks that judgements of this sort are always "judgements about possibilities". In fact, they are judgements made defeasibly, rather than relating to what is possible, as though hypothetical in some sense. Given the satisfaction of the initial conditions, and the absence of any challenge, the defeasible relation offers us a guarantee. Furthermore, the burden of proof is typically on the objector, and this is as we expect: you must prove that your client is a kleptomaniac in order to have him declared "not fit to plead" [KEY CASE 2] while I have no such obligation (he counts as an agent unless you show he is not).

An example: *Sophie's Choice*

When discussing one another as agents, appraising actions morally, etc., we are neither doing nor trying to do (natural) science: causal accounts are (often) inappropriate (as the two-language view recognized). For actions (at least), descriptions are defeasible, rather than importing a *ceteris paribus* clause. We need not consider all counter-possibilities. Further, any causal accounts here could not necessitate since no complete specification of the content of the *ceteris paribus* clause could be supplied (even in principle) and since (the topic for the next section) we have no reason to conceive of causation as generally exceptionless or necessitating , a conception appropriate to natural science (see p. 127).

To put my "solution" bluntly, consider the film *Sophie's Choice* (1982). Here, the Meryl Streep character has to choose which of her two children will be adopted by a Nazi family (and therefore be likely to survive), and which child goes to the concentration camp and likely death. In the film, the choice Sophie makes is explicable: we can see the predicament of a Jewish woman and her children, during World War Two, in Hitler's Europe, and so on. We recognize the pressures that require her to choose in this ghastly situation. Yet is Sophie's actual choice inevitable? We might voice this concern by asking if *we* would have chosen differently. Now, that question has a point only for someone in a relevantly similar situation. But which are the relevant similarities? What is the weight of the woman's being, say, Jewish, given that Hitler's Europe was horrible for gypsies also? What is the weight of it being the mother who faces the terrible choice rather than, for instance, (two different cases) the father or an aunt? (And so on, for various aspects of the case.) There are no clear answers here. We might understand what "caused" this woman in this situation to make this choice, but have we a basis for moving beyond such specificities? Surely we have reason to suppose that we do not: that her choice is necessarily specific. As we have seen, it is impossible to fill in all the details of that *ceteris paribus* clause; therefore, there is no hope of producing a causal "law" that could then be used in other cases; for example, in my case.

Suppose that, in discussing the film, I say, "In her position, I would have done the same". This is plausibly true, as long as I am being honest, and so on. But, at best, this is not causally necessitated, but rather made true by the way the explanation is constructed: were I in her rough position, and yet chose differently, that would show that I was not in her precise position. (All the things that had to be equal were not equal – or I must choose the same way she did: that is the force of *ceteris paribus* here.) But this does not imply that she did not choose: rather, we could only write the "causal" principle here with hindsight, when we know what she in fact chose. We could not know what the outcome would be. So we cannot determine any principle's applicability in my case. These "causes" do not necessitate in the way we had earlier taken them to.

This discussion seems to imply that there is some specific situation in which the woman, Sophie, finds herself – some situation whose specification (and hence whose specificity) includes descriptions of Sophie herself – such that, if I found myself in that situation, I would (or would not) act as she did. But this assumption of completeness is misplaced in two related ways (as we saw), reflecting two assumptions of determinism: namely, that there is a finite totality of possibilities and that descriptions of the world form a coherent "package" (at least in principle); that an "absolute conception of the world" (Williams 1985: 139) is possible. Or, to put that a different way (used earlier: p. 112), that the descriptions of various parts or aspects of the world might, in principle, be conjoined. Once these assumptions are dropped, imagining a case otherwise like Sophie's lacks any "predictive" force from knowing how she chose in this one case. For we cannot use her case (her decision) as a basis for prediction without assuming what is at issue; namely, that we are relevantly like her.

Causal laws: another look?

One consequence of the argument of Chapter 4, perhaps not one explicitly noted, was that a free will defence cannot be founded on the counter-causal: that we must accept that every event has a cause. Yet it might seem that (in denying the necessitating function of the causal), I am really denying *causality*. Such a conclusion would weaken this line of defence against the determinist argument, by removing our account of the insight of determinism.

Any argument here must also recognize the universal applicability of scientific explanation; a mode of explanation that is certainly primarily causal. Human behaviour too can be given causal explanation. Yet the determinist argument requires not merely the causality urged in the first premise of the argument but also the *necessity* claimed for causal explanation in premise 4. But causal arguments *not* part of the scientific are not always necessitating. Explanations in the "social sciences" are often causal in just this sense (p. 133): giving some quasi-predictive power, but without the implication of some covering law. In fact, and more commonly, when we look for explanations that do not necessitate, the mode will not be causal. Yet, for action, we have granted a causal substrate (Chapter 6, p. 95) in the movements (or non-movements) that comprise that action. And our concern here is with that causal story.

But when are causes necessitating? Or, when do we ask questions (or raise issues) requiring causal answers of this sort? The quick response has two forms: (a) when we decide to, by introducing some *ceteris paribus* clause, or (b) when we are doing (natural) science. As we will see, these quick responses come together.

Emphasizing the inexorability of causality presents something fundamental to the issue, explaining why it still raises its head, despite our strong sense of ourselves as agents. In the case of billiard balls [KEY CASE 8], we expect a different outcome to reflect a difference in the initial conditions: there must have been such a difference, or there would have been the same outcome! This seems to reinstate *causal necessity*: in fact, the upshot is that we provide the "inexorability" of causal laws as they apply in natural science, by not permitting "deviation". To proceed differently would not be to engage in science. Thus we make this assumption of "inexorability" for the natural world, and the project of science warrants just such an assumption. But we do not make it for *action*. So that science builds in the assumption that there is one ultimate description; therefore that is the appropriate way to behave when one is doing science. But there are other occasions!

Thus the necessitating force of causality is present only in some circumstances: roughly, when approaching certain issues or questions, characteristically those of natural science. (So, when my doctor asks me about my condition, or explains it, the relevant explanations are causally necessitating (when correct) even if some others are not.) Thus seeing causal descriptions as ways of responding to the issues raised in scientific enquiries will recognize Hampshire's "inexhaustibility of descriptions" (p. 121) even for causal descriptions. Then the slogan "Every event has a cause" means that all occurrences viewed as *events* will be explicable scientifically: nothing (that is, no event) escapes science (Best 1978: 90–93).

Must one know the causal laws? No. One's commitment is to there *being* such a law (Searle 1983: 113 note: compare Davidson 1980: 18) – this is just one's commitment to the project of twentieth-century science. And, of course, just the same problem here recurs for non-human as for human events: one does not have to know why it snows to be committed to the snow's being causally explicable. But this thought helps us see what the determinist has right: the *inexorability* of laws in the natural sciences.

So the necessity in causation is not something we discover, some empirical fact. Rather, it represents a commitment on our parts: to treat causal explanations (especially those in natural science) as necessitating and exceptionless. In doing so, we recognize that causal laws only necessitate *ceteris paribus* since, if the initial conditions differ, the "cause" itself (the "antecedent state of the world": Chapter 2, p. 21) would be different. Yet (as we have seen: p. 118) we do not (and cannot) check all the characteristics of those "initial conditions": there is no finite totality of them. And when the question concerns causality in natural science, the conditions to be controlled-for will typically be given by the relevant theory, and hence be implicit.

To put that another way, the idea is that, whereas "laws" are often not conformed to,[7] *exceptions* will be explicable in terms intelligible from the basic theory: so that, if we have "exceptions" to Newton's First Law of Motion, these do not count as genuine exceptions, since they reflect differences of "initial conditions". So, in the context of natural science, to be exceptionless is for there to be no *inexplicable* exceptions. Finding that the results of a particular experiment do not conform to the natural law, we should conclude that, contrary to our first thought, either the initial conditions or the relevant laws are not what we thought they were. That is what the term "exceptionless" means in this context. Further, this conclusion is founded on the principle that there will be no exceptions to well founded laws of natural science: finding genuine exceptions would be conceding that the putative laws did not really describe the world around us (and looking for new laws).

This point is best seen by considering the factors we control for in formulating an experimental protocol. For example, an experiment aimed at studying human gait might ensure that each subject was fully into his or her stride pattern before measurement takes place. The rationale would be that constancy in the results presupposes that what is studied is the *regular* stride, not some irregular or abnormal stride. So here we are controlling for the factor of irregularity of stride-pattern. Such factors, then, must be controlled for because they would otherwise raise questions about the reliability of the results.

First, such factors provide a (theoretical?) grounding for what needs to be considered and offer a basis for rejecting apparent counter-cases. For instance, in line with the first idea, in performing an experiment in our physics laboratory, we do not typically control for the gravitational effect of the moon, even though we accept (a) that the moon has a gravitational effect on every piece of apparatus (from Newton's "laws"); and (b) the necessity of "controlling" for the moon's gravitational effects if our study concerned tides. But why should we do this in one case and not the other? The answer is given both by the theoretical account of the scale of the relevant effects and by the theoretical understanding that, if the effects that can apply will apply equally to all our apparatus (within limits of our concern with, say, measurement), we do not need to consider them.

Second, manifest in such "controlling" for variables (say, initial conditions) is our commitment to the laws or principles as necessitating, which then allows us to deal with apparent counter-instances. If we grant the truth of some causal principle (say, that water boils at 100°C) then we must explain away cases where this does not seem to be so, but still preserve the generality of the principle. Faced with a beaker of water manifestly boiling at some other temperature (or at that temperature yet not boiling), the principle would be reformulated, highlighting ways of explaining away this case. For example, if we get any pure water, at the standard pressure, in an open vessel (which is smooth inside, without being too smooth), etc., then water will boil at 100°C. So we are not tolerating exceptions to the "law". Thus "controlling for" includes specifying which of the "other things" (the *cetera*) one requires to be equal to count as a genuine trial, and rejecting apparent exceptions; at least, rejecting (as failing the first condition) cases that might otherwise falsify "truths" of science.

As above, rather than give up the claim that water boils at 100°C, we assert that, say, this was not pure water (and criticize the experimental procedure employed). Thus, if the motion of the earth or the moon's gravitational effect were relevant to a particular experiment, but were not controlled for (say, because unnoticed), the results of that experiment could not provide counter-evidence against some putative "law of nature": indeed, we explain away the results by pointing out the failure to control for whatever it was.

One of the "contextualizations" of causal situations involves treating them as wholly general: but every actual situation is specific in a number of relevant ways. When doing natural science, we "bracket" such differences in line with the various commitments of the natural science (say, physics). And one such will be the idea of a uniformity of nature: that the same processes apply everywhere. But, for contemporary science at least, the uniformity of nature really amounts to the uniformity of laws: that the same laws apply everywhere. Then, too, the "neatness" of such laws is provided by their mathematical formulation (Feynman 1992 [1965]: 36–54): hence it really amounts to a commitment to the uniformity of mathematical expression, where mathematics provides both neatness and inexorability. Causal explanations in science are inexorable because we treat them that way, and brook no contradiction.

Of course, the above discussion is entirely concerned with explanations in natural science. A quite general constraint on our discussion of free will was that we illustrate, not merely that the determinist account of causation was wrong in its full generality, but that causes in natural science *did* necessitate. Further, the reference to natural science is essential: how, if at all, any of this relates to social science (and hence the nature of social science) should remain an open question.[8] And this exclusion is justified by our concern (see Chapter 2, p. 27) with the strongest version of the determinist thesis. Moreover, to find causal necessity here is, of course, not to find it generally: as we have seen, where we do not import the assumptions of natural science, we are not entitled to the *ceteris paribus* clauses required to make sense of the idea of a finite totality of possibilities or of the conjoinability of descriptions.

To see the point, as earlier for Sophie's choice (p. 125), note that causal explanations are often given after the fact. But this important idea[9] might be understood in two rather different ways. There is a trivial sense, which recognizes that X could not be the *cause* of Y unless there is a Y (unless Y occurred). And so X cannot be designated as the cause of *Y* until *Y* has occurred (Chapter 6, p. 81). But this really says nothing; for two reasons. First, *X or Z* can be sufficient to cause *Y*, without knowing which was the cause of *Y* in this case: so it makes sense to ask about (and hence to attribute) causal power, even if counterfactually, by talking about what did not cause *Y* this time, although it might next time. Second, we can think of causal laws operating predictively: "If *X*, then *Y*". What if there had never been any previous cases of *X*?

Still, we are happy that if that boulder had fallen, then the river would have been dammed because we know about more general effects of boulders on rivers. (Still, the "inexhaustibility of description" (see p. 122) might raise questions here.) But even this feature can be important since we do not know for sure, independent of what happens, what there is to explain.

A more interesting version takes the causal relation to only be *identifiable* after the fact. How might we make this out? In practice, we typically identify *X* as the cause of *Y* because *X* makes the difference. If everything else had been the same, but *X* absent, *Y* would not have occurred: "when the magnetic field was not turned on, the stream of electrons was not deflected, but it was deflected when the magnetic field was on: therefore the magnetic field is the cause of the deflection". This suggests that we can only identify causes by seeing what makes the difference in this way, but, as we saw (Chapter 2, p. 24), this is not a thesis against the determinist. Were many other features of the situation absent, the outcome would have been different. (It is for this reason that the determinist thinks of the antecedent state of the world (including *X*) as the cause of *Y*.) The relevant causal law states, say, that if *X* occurs then *Y* will occur: but, of course, there is an implicit background here, provided by the theoretical "laden-ness" (Chalmers 1999: 7–9, 14–18) of observations or experiments relevant here. This means that, in the future, a similar *X* will cause a similar *Y ceteris paribus*: and we have seen the sense in which such a conclusion should not be thought to support determinism.

Causal explanation and the social

But what about elsewhere, outside science? In effect, the sorts of cases required as examples here identify causal interests that differ from those of natural science. Earlier (p. 119) we saw how an interest in a table as provider of a solid surface (to support beer glasses) differed from an interest in its molecular structure, as "atomic" points and spaces, but both were acknowledged as *causal* interests. Yet (causal) interest other than that of natural science did not, in the same way, stress necessity as built into causal relations. Rather, its focus was on particular (causal) situations: the ability of this table, now, to support this glass of beer (and predictions for its later good service in the same task). Of course, one could argue that the descriptions must be conjoinable with those of, say, the physics of the table, but why *should* one do so? What (apart from a prior theoretical commitment, of the kind mentioned earlier) could drive us to this conclusion? There is no such reason. We have causality here without conjoining, by recognizing the context-specificity of the questions or issues our causal "stories" address.

For the kleptomaniac [KEY CASE 2], the causal story is necessitating: but there are specific reasons in this case. The term "kleptomaniac" contrasts that person with the rest of us (in this respect). Our acceptance of this idea of kleptomania commits us to such a contrast. In a similar vein, the doctor who prescribes certain pills is, for those purposes, treating me as a physical system, governed by causal necessity: if the diagnosis is correct, and the pills (and the dosage) the appropriate ones for my condition, that condition will be alleviated (or cured, or whatever). But the assumption here is that a relevantly similar person with a relevantly similar condition can also be helped. And (as the use of the term "relevantly similar" indicates) this is *exceptionless*: someone who was not helped by those pills would have a different condition, or require a larger dosage, or . . .. So the pills will work *ceteris paribus*. Here we have the classic connection of causal necessity to complete description and *ceteris paribus*. Further, the doctor only treats me as a causal system for some purposes. He or she grants that I can take the medication at the prescribed times, and such like. So here too there is an implicit contextualization of the causal necessities.

In this case, then, the doctor treats me, as patient, causally and takes causes to necessitate: if the pills really are the appropriate ones for my condition, that condition will be cured, or whatever. In this respect, medicine is operating as a natural science. Social sciences differ. One feature regularly referred to is that *experiments* are not possible in, say, sociology or economics (as they are not in history).[10] This is partly explained as a moral prohibition on the kinds of experimentation appropriate to human subjects (which, of course, implicitly acknowledges them as agents) and partly on the individuality of human situations. We cannot experiment since we cannot completely replicate a situation, and cannot "sort out" which conditions to "control for"[11], so no prediction in this area could be exceptionless. We cannot know in *advance* which characteristics of the situation will be the relevant ones. At best, we focus on the likely ones, the ones we might "bet on", and, with a good explanatory or predictive model, we would expect to find few exceptions, few cases in need of special explanation. Indeed, that is what it means to call the model "good". As Nagel eloquently puts it: "The central subject of economics is human motivation in the aggregate: how the decisions, rational and irrational, of millions of people combine to produce large-scale results" (1995: 183). But "laws" for such a subject will not (typically) be exceptionless. Moreover, while the best of such laws (or "models") do indeed have a high predictive power (although, for our purposes, the mere possibility of such power suffices), a high degree of predictiveness here is not exceptionless.[12]

From the perspective of such social sciences, even explanations of bodily movements will not be causally necessitating if, say, their explanation lies in economics. Rather, like remarks about "the average English family", they will be made true by being generally true. The "laws" of economics are not, in that sense, causal laws! (Better, perhaps, to say that causal laws for human behaviour are not exceptionless, and do not support causal necessity.)

So explanations of social phenomena, even when viewed broadly causally, could not manifest the law-likeness that the determinist requires for causal necessity. In effect, this is partly the harvest from arguments in Chapter 3 (p. 50): the difficulties of drawing up psychological "laws" in this sense means that psychological determinism can never be as powerful a position as determinism based on physical causation, because physical causation lends itself to just these laws (at least, when addressing questions of kinds posed in the natural sciences).

Thus causal descriptions, too, typically function as answers to a particular kind of question, either explicitly (when the question is asked) or implicitly, where the context of investigation clarifies the nature of the question at issue. Asked about the movement of billiard ball *A* after its collision with billiard ball *B* [KEY CASE 8], one does not, as a general rule, check for meteorites in the vicinity, unless this is the meteorite season, or some favoured landing site. In the context of the question, it is not to the point to do so. Any answer is not rendered *incomplete* by failure to check for meteorites, just as when I urge that a cheetah can run faster than a man I do not check on whether the cheetah's legs are broken. In the context of my assertion, that is simply not at issue. And anyone disputing my assertions must find a reason in *this* case for his or her objection: the relations here are *defeasible*.

Those who think that the causal sequence will not work out as initially described are "empowered" to raise this "head of exception". But it must be raised as more than a mere possibility: as something that might occur. Rather, some reason to think that, in this case, it will be realized must be offered. So one would investigate the meteorite possibility if this were the meteorite season and the billiard table a favoured landing spot.

Further, causal descriptions are of use only if they are the appropriate ones in a particular context. A person offering a causal description in an inappropriate context is not offering something true and then of questionable *relevance*, nor something that could supersede action-description, nor even that competes with it, but rather (in the context of that question or issue) something irrelevant. He or she is like the husband in the earlier example [KEY CASE 12](Chapter 6, p. 91) who says he was drunk because he had consumed ten pints of beer, or equally like the person who gives the six decimal place answer about the table's length when the problem at hand is to move the table through a doorway [KEY CASE 15]. Discussing choice, to talk about causes, and really mean *causes*, is to be rambling on, beside the point.

How is such appropriateness to be explained? For reasons we have seen (in particular, the "inexhaustibility of description", p. 122), there are many kinds of appropriateness, tied to the different concerns humans might have. Hence no general answer can be attempted. With a large number of purposes, we have a large number of *speaking-sensitive* occasions for the asking of apparently (but not actually) the same questions (p. 123). Thus, the drunken husband above [KEY CASE 12] fails to distinguish the issue his wife raises with the question, "Why are you drunk?" from issues the biologist might raise in those same words. Here the same form of words asks different questions or raises different issues. Equally, asking teenagers the way to a particular local landmark may, for success, require a vocabulary different from that used to enquire from the local police. So different forms of words ask the same question or raise the same issue.

This latter point is our bulwark against one major danger: of seeming to prove too much; of attributing freedom too generally, to tables, etc. Our answer has both emphasized the restricted purposes of questions asked in the "hard sciences" (or to which those sciences provide answers) and acknowledged that, within that compass (which includes the tables, billiard balls, etc.), causal questions and explanations will typically be the appropriate ones.

Conclusion

Is what I have defended really *free will*? Adopting my conclusions gives reasons to reject the determinist argument: if these reasons too are accepted, there will be no principled basis to reject free will, since the determinist argument provides the only basis for such a rejection (see Chapter 9). Of course, the conception of free will thereby defended is only one on which the *possibility* of agency is at issue: it does not imply any wide range of real options for persons. In this sense, then, the conclusion establishes, say, my responsibility for walking across the room or sitting down (in at least some cases). It does not offer specific hope of my becoming the managing director of a major multinational company or of leading a proletarian revolution (however much I may want to do either thing).

But what counter-blasts might the determinist offer to my argument? Three suggest themselves, with determinists making the following claims:

1. The argument does not do its job – does not show the claimed connection to *ceteris paribus* clauses, etc.
2. The argument proves too much – it gets rid of causality.
3. The argument is not sound – it does not get rid of the determinist conclusion.

The first line of objection is met by rehearsing the impact of *ceteris paribus* clauses on the determinist's own position. We have seen how the determinists explain away deviation from the expectation of what typically happens: rightly in the case of explanations in the natural sciences, mistakenly elsewhere.

The second objection is explicitly met above: my commitment to causality is reinforced by my account of its place, especially in respect of explanations in the natural sciences, and its associated necessity (in those contexts). I have been keen to insist that causality, and even causal necessity, within scientific explanation is preserved by this conclusion: indeed, a constraint of the account of free action (introduced in Chapter 4) is to preserve *both* universal causation and the causal structures of science. For, far from saving free will, the counter-causal seems its death. But, drawing on the two-language view, I have been at pains to stress the *context-sensitivity* – the sensitivity to issue, in particular – that can characterize causal explanations (as others).

The discussion here should meet the third line of objection, that concerning whether the conclusion of determinism might be true even if/although the determinist argument (as I have reconstructed it: Chapter 2, p. 21) is rejected. Four related matters of central importance take us into Chapter 9. First, as a point of logic, the conclusion of any argument may be true even if the argument itself is not sound: from the fact that we have no argument for a conclusion, we cannot infer that the conclusion is not *true*. However, and second, without that argument we have no basis for accepting the conclusion; no reason to give it "house room", as it were. Now, we urged (Chapter 2, p. 28) that this argument generated the most powerful determinism: that any other argument would imply *less*. Were this acknowledged, third, we would have reason to doubt that a comparable argument for this conclusion should be found. Finally, we have at least some reason to doubt the conclusion of the determinist argument: not only is it counter-intuitive to suggest that there is no such thing as *choice*, and not only have we our positive remarks on the nature of choosing and explaining, but we have the difficulty in articulating the determinist conclusion independently of the premises involved in that argument. As we might put it, the argument itself shows us how those ideas are to be appropriately understood. We will see, in Chapter 9, that this permits another way to reformulate our overall argument, by identifying the problem of determinism as a problem for philosophy.

Conclusions and reflections 9 on philosophical method

The argument of the book is now complete. We have explored a number of traditional options concerning free action (that is, canvassed alternatives to determinism) having first set out a determinist argument as a way of posing the issue. In passing, the philosophical strategies of argument have been highlighted. In both these ways, then, this text is a suitable "beginners' guide" to philosophical investigations of this traditional topic.

I have put forward a "solution" (better, a dissolution) of the problem. Here I tie up some loose ends by commenting both on that solution and on the strategy of the book (p. 139), saying a little more, of a general kind, about the nature of that "solution" (p. 137) and discussing briefly its location in the frame of free will defences (p. 139). It also includes a remark on an issue not taken as central here, although regularly discussed in books on the freedom of the will: the idea of *control* (p. 148).

Context-sensitivity and explanation

It is worth stressing the contextual weight of my "answer": my free will defence relies on contrasting "utterances" in terms of their occasion-sensitive features. When we assume both the applicability of *ceteris paribus* clauses and the applicability of causal explanation, the determinist conclusion is warranted. And this is our position when doing natural science. But we are not so disposed, nor should we be, in respect of human behaviour (even viewed as movement). For now the impossibility of filling-out the *ceteris paribus* clauses (demonstrated in Chapter 8) must make us hesitant about the *general* usefulness of explanatory pictures that such require clauses.

Yet to deny the general applicability of such models or pictures is both to accept that view for natural science and yet to admit causal explanations that are not exceptionless. As we have seen (Chapter 8, p. 133), some generalizations in social science seem to have exactly this character:[1] although there is, say, no "iron law" of economics (which, for instance, necessitates in respect of economic predictions), that does not render useless those predictions, viewed as "a good bet" or even "the best bet". They may both provide a reliable basis for decisions and an explanatory framework. For instance, someone designing a water-sports complex for the children of the region would have a basis for planning if he or she knew the average number of children in families in that area together with the total number of families with children. At least he or she would know the maximum "target audience". He or she could then consider, say, the average disposable income of these families, and again get useful information to factor into the planning. No particular family has precisely that disposable income and that number of children (2.2!), and some families have no interest in water sports. Neither of these facts is denied in the calculations. The relevant "laws" that generate the generalizations are not exceptionless. But giving weight to a prediction is justified in such a case even though its "law" permitted exceptions. As Nagel eloquently remarked (quoted Chapter 8, p. 133): "The central subject of economics is human motivation in the aggregate: how the decisions, rational and irrational, of millions of people combine to produce large-scale results" (1995: 183). Yet, since "laws" of such a subject will not be exceptionless, they are a species of generalization.[2] Indeed, if the choice were between such generalizations and the introduction of a *ceteris paribus* clause (with its implications), we should prefer that first option – for reasons sketched in Chapter 8.

I conclude that the contextualist rejection of the *ubiquitousness* of causal necessity is, at the least, a plausible strategy here.

What kind of "free will defence"?

How should my defence of free will be classified? Certainly it is not a libertarian view: it does not deny (indeed, it affirms) universal causation. Still, in rejecting the generality of causal necessity, it owes something to libertarianism (see especially MacKay 1967). Indeed, the rejection of "the possibility of a complete description" (Passmore 1966: 330) has been attributed to Heisenberg as a thesis within science (compare Chapter 4). Be that as it may, such *incompleteness* is not typically a feature of scientific explanation: the implication that complete description is impossible is there defeated by the introduction of *ceteris paribus* clauses, and by a commitment to exceptionless laws. I have added an explanation both of why this thesis might be thought to rebut determinism without doing so (it proves too much if thought of as a basis for a free will defence); and why, properly understood, a parallel thesis in the philosophy of understanding actually does offer elements for a dissolution of the determinist argument.

Equally, my account is not straightforwardly compatibilist, since its argument grants that, having acknowledged the movement/action contrast, the determinist might still derive the substance of his or her conclusions by focusing on (bodily) movements only, including omissions. Yet the spirit of my account is indeed compatibilist: that the determinist's insights bypass his or her conclusions.

So this position does not lend itself to categorisation within the framework (identified in Chapter 4) of the traditional arguments against the determinist conclusion. However, it is precisely an argument against adoption of that conclusion, based on the (principled) rejection of a crucial premise (premise 4) of the determinist argument. Here I have shown both the *crucial* nature of this premise to the determinist and the error that premise embodies (viewed generally). Equally, I have illustrated (and clarified) the insights that motivate determinism.

The strategy of the book

Looking back, with the twenty-twenty vision of hindsight, the strategy in the book can be summarized in three stages:

1. Question: For whom is the question of free will a (live) issue? Answer: For philosophers.
2. Question: Why is it (even) an issue for philosophers? Answer: Because of the determinist argument – if there were no determinist argument, even philosophers would not be perplexed.
3. Therefore, meeting the determinist argument (in its strongest form) is establishing the freedom of the will by removing any (plausible) basis for philosophers to deny it.

Nothing that I have written here establishes the viability of the first of these moves: indeed, my introduction of the problem might have led others to expect that I would find "free will issues" in many other places. Before addressing that point (p. 141), however, it is worth commenting on all three steps, by way of clarification.

With regard to the first, the thought is two-fold: that speaking "with the vulgar"[3] there is no real issue, because, from our perspective, we are clearly agents. In this respect, it is "a scandal for philosophy" (Kant 1996 [1787]: B xl: 36 n.144; see Stroud 1984: 128) but not elsewhere. Further, others might be *misled* into thinking there was an issue here by mistaking philosophers' questions for their own, so that what we must do is "battle against the bewitchment of our intelligence by means of language" (Wittgenstein 1953: §109[4]).

The second strategic move has been visible throughout this text: we have kept "the determinist argument" steadily in our sights, while admitting that there is not just *one* such argument; rather, we have concentrated on what we argued to be the most powerful form of that argument. Of course, finding no *reason* to be a determinist would not show that determinism was false but should put the "burden of proof" on the defender of determinism. And then, given some of the implausibilities mentioned earlier (see Chapter 3), the "best explanation" will surely be to reject the determinist conclusion.

The third move picks up two key points: if, as urged earlier in Chapter 8, the determinist argument is flawed, even those concerned with philosophical matters have no reason to be determinists – but, further, that does not mean that we must establish some counter-causal freedom, nor explain how persons are agents.

An issue for philosophers?

For Kant, it was a scandal for philosophy that the existence of an external world could not be demonstrated. If there were no philosophers, the perplexity Kant was concerned with would not arise. Only once we are concerned with, in this case, "some very general understanding of how [human] . . . knowledge is possible" (Stroud 1984: 129), a concern characteristic of philosophy, would we be perplexed about the existence of the external world *tout court*, as opposed to attempting to determine whether I am hallucinating the wall in front of my speeding car (that is, with a *particular* puzzle).

The problems of the common-sense sceptic, for instance, derive from cases where doubt about our knowledge-claims seem justified: for example, our (perceptual) knowledge of objects that are very small, or far away (Descartes 1984 [1641]: 12), or seen under peculiar lighting conditions. And scepticism of this sort needs no independent justification: it is merely being careful in what we claim to know. By contrast, the philosophical sceptic raises questions concerning (in this example) *all* perceptual claims (Dilman 1975: 106–8), where doubt is raised despite our having what we call "the very best evidence": is it really good evidence at all? Now, *such* scepticism must be justified. We need more than mere caution to raise it for consideration. It might, for instance, be motivated in two stages. First, we can urge the general principle that, for any knowledge-claim, other possibilities consistent with the evidence-base must be ruled-out (Stroud 1984: 27–30). For example, I do not *know* there is a goldfinch in the garden if all my "evidence" is consistent with the bird being a goldcrest (Austin 1970: 83–8). Then, second, we can urge that this condition cannot be met; for example, by raising the possibility that my supposed evidence might all be dreamed. There are two points to notice here: (a) the generality characteristic of the philosophical issue (Scruton 1994: 3–4) and (b) the need to motivate that issue. These must be met in our case.

Consider the argument in "a landmark in the history of criminal law" (Cahn 1972: 75). Two young men, Nathan Leopold and Richard Loeb, were accused of (and confessed to) the murder of a cousin of Loeb's, Bobby Franks.[5] At the 1924 trial, the defence lawyer, Clarence Darrow, appeared to argue wholly generally: "I know that any one of an infinite number of causes reaching back to the beginning might be working out in these boys' minds" (Darrow 1957: 37, quoted in Cahn 1972: 76). He went on to draw the general conclusion: "We are all helpless" (Darrow 1957: 37, quoted in Cahn 1972: 76).

Roughly, then, Darrow's argument is that Leopold and Loeb *could not* have done otherwise than they did: that their behaviour was (causally) determined by "forces" in their psychologies. So that the outcome was inevitable, given also the way the other circumstances came together. This must mean that Leopold and Loeb were both *bound* to feel the way they did (given those circumstances) and *bound* to act in that way.

But, although there is a similar story about the development of our minds, which involves education and other psychological "influences", such a general conclusion is not warranted. Certainly, in this set of circumstances, Leopold and Loeb were bound to behave in these ways. These two men, given their specific social situations, couldn't do otherwise than they did: the "compulsion" of Leopold and Loeb reflects the way in which their previous lives had led them in certain directions, and the sense in which their choices had become constrained. But we take the situations in their cases to be *distinctive*, and then cite the unusual characteristics of those upbringings. For example, one was put (by his parents) into an all-girls school. Such factors represent the "heads of exception" (Chapter 8, p. 124) raised in these cases, and justify us contrasting this case with the "'usual" situation.

Our standard (common-sense or practical) problems for free will are those typified by the Leopold and Loeb case. Here we are offered specific reasons to doubt the freedom of the "actions" of these persons: we are given reason to doubt that, in this case, there was genuine agency (or, perhaps, full agency). But this resembles the cases used by the common-sense sceptic: the doubt does not generalize. Indeed, one might think of this as the central insight from Strawson's discussion (Chapter 7, p. 102): that we can regard the behaviour of others as determined only when we see them as "incapacitated in some or all respects for ordinary personal relationships" (P. Strawson 1974: 12).

As the example of scepticism articulated above suggests, the generality of the free will problem arises only by raising philosophical doubts; for only they have the required generality. And this is just to apply the first point above, the need for generality, to this case.

Now, my position is that, in a parallel with the second point above, concerning motivating, the free will issue is only motivated by the determinist argument: that, without that argument, we have no basis for an issue of such generality as the philosophical issue requires.

So, according to my view, the free will issue is only an issue for philosophy: with no philosophical perplexity, it would disappear. And, as urged above, that perplexity is the consequence of the determinist argument. But were there no other parties genuinely perplexed about free action? In this section and the next two, we first consider parallel cases to highlight the idea of an issue for philosophy, meet an objection to the cogency of our response as a "solution" and then describe the pedigree of the conception of philosophy at work here.

Who is perplexed about, say, the existence of the external world? Well, no doubt some students of philosophy become perplexed, listening to their tutors. (Some students are always perplexed by tutors, of course.) But only if struck by the philosophical issues in general would one make such a perplexity one's own. For this reason, Kant rightly characterizes it as a problem "for philosophy" (Kant 1996 [1787]: B xl) that the existence of the external world has not been demonstrated: only philosophers would think this a suitable topic for demonstration, or understand demonstration in this way (*more geometrico*).

To apply, both the *terms* of the debate about free action and the *issues* it encompasses are philosophers' constructs. The second case is easier to see (and is approached in this section). For, to generate a determinist conclusion, one must deny the *possibility* of action, not merely highlight limitations of action: indeed, to recognize limitations on action is to concede the possibility of agency. If we think about some theorist being perplexed about the freedom of a particular action, the answer as to its freedom is typically forthcoming. Well, the grounds for that answer are clear, even when the details are not. For we know, as it were, the grounds on which the presumption of agency might be defeated: in this case, he was compelled; in that case, she was coerced; there it was the result of post-hypnotic suggestion; here of drug or disease; and so on. And it is right to see here the presumption of agency: that the very setting-up of the question about the freedom of this or that action imports the idea that some actions are, typically, free; that we need only consider the exceptional cases. Moreover, in seeing themselves as able to consider these exceptional cases, the lawyers or psychologists presuppose the very idea of agency. They simply dispute its *application* to some case. Yet this is precisely not identifying a problem for philosophy. The philosophical problem only arises when we step back from these *minutiae*, looking for some more general characterization. And why should one do this? The answer for philosophers (but not others) is: because one is faced with the determinist argument.

A rough parallel here may be informative. Consider, for example, someone who urges that what pass for reasons are not really reasons but, instead (mere) rationalizations. Such a thesis could be interpreted in two different ways. The first is as a remark pertaining to some offered reason, as when someone asserts that, although I said I became a philosophy teacher to disseminate understanding of philosophy, that was not my *reason* but a (mere) rationalization. And such a conversation continues by specifying my real reason: say, my belief that philosophy conferences were a good place to meet attractive women. Here, there is no general scepticism about reason. Rather, there is doubt that what is offered as a reason in this case is the real reason. The other interpretation is "reasons" scepticism: nothing would count as a reason here. But this second view is untenable; and two considerations (two reasons, we might say) can be given. First, that claim to scepticism must itself be supported, for otherwise why should we accept it? Yet to support it is to offer reasons. Second, the contrast between a reason and a rationalization is undermined by this thesis, yet it is a thesis that employs just this contrast.

One crucial feature here, though, is that such general scepticism is not the province of those actively concerned about the practice of reasoning: say, the particular reasoning of historians. Rather, it is the province of abstract concerns; of philosophy.

To apply: objections to the freedom of action can take the form of denying that this or that particular action is free. Here, a free will defender could readily concede the point, for what is thereby undermined is just the assumption *in this case*, and that very move concedes the possibility of freedom in other cases (and that is the free will defence).

Notice, too, that the worries of lawyers or psychologists about free will are typically of this type: whether some person is free (for example, Leopold and Loeb). Yet putting the worry this way still implicitly concedes freedom of action in typical cases, with which the cases under consideration are implicitly contrasted. And these are *not* the worries generated, as in this text, via the determinist argument.

The other "reading" of the opposition to free action is that which is sceptical about free will *as such*: and, as we saw initially (Chapter 1, p. 7), this amounts to scepticism about the possibility of action. Yet such scepticism must be motivated. (Here, there is no straightforward refutation.) My policy has been to motivate such scepticism with my determinist argument (Chapter 2, p. 21). Such a strategy can only have "bite" where sceptical issues in general have "bite"; and that is on philosophers.

To illustrate, consider three cases where, pre-theoretically, one might assume that freedom of action was at issue. In all of them, we find that the concern is with the *range* of (free) action, not its possibility. These have been chosen both as powerful candidates for areas of concern and as highlighting the kinds of responses appropriate in such cases. Further, and in line with Strawson's insight (Chapter 7, p. 102), all are cases to be distinguished from the usual.

First, as we have seen, lawyers assume agency: they contrast the kleptomaniac [KEY CASE 2] with other people – with "the rest of us". So the implicit requirement is for the possibility of agency, with that presumption defeated in such cases as the kleptomaniac. Further, they assume that their own activities, say, as litigators, are to be understood as agency; and hence as praise-worthy (and rewarded accordingly). At best, then, their issue concerns the scope of freedom in selected cases: so there is no general problem about free will here; nor could there be.

Second, and similarly, psychologists assume the possibility of action, at least on the part of psychologists themselves (and also in those patients who come to them, from whom they take money, etc.). There may be a vexed question here (as there was for Freud: see Dilman 1984: 163) about how psychology is possible in a world of universal causality – how it does not simply collapse into neuro-physiology – but *that* it does not is taken for granted. Of course, this fact is clouded both by the tendency of some writers on psychology to mix psychological and physiological language without seeming to notice (Hobson 1988: 292) and by the concern of some psychologists to consider pathologies, where (arguably) there might be "unfreedom", in ways that actually reinforce their commitment to the free will of "the rest of us": for example, cases of post-hypnotic suggestion.

Third, some religious believers assert a determinist thesis. Now these come in too many varieties for all to be discussed here,[6] but, broadly, they can be categorized in two groups. The first group is those for whom there is a philosophical question about the nature of agency. But they are likely to be amenable to the sorts of argument deployed here (perhaps augmented by one treating the so-called problem of evil (Kenny 1992b: 77–83)). The second group take some form of determinism as an act of faith, but then, if they assume at least divine agency, they are again discussing the scope, rather than the possibility, of agency.

To bring out the point here, let us ask: whose perplexity remains unaddressed by what posing *their own* questions assumes? The lawyers and the psychologists assume (at least) their own freedom of action: hence they assume the possibility of agency, and then their primary concerns (when raising issues of "free will") might be when that agency is attenuated or reduced. So, of course, they do not know what to make of perplexing cases. Maybe there is nothing *in general* to make of them: maybe they can only be considered case-by-case.

No doubt the case of religious believers is rather different. But, given the interpenetration of philosophical issues with (some) religious ones (and given the context of a broadly secular society), I should not be too daunted if this was the only case that seemed problematic.

Another revealing case that might seem to make a free will problem more than just an issue for philosophers would be this:[7] I portray myself as a victim of my circumstances and my body. "Take me as I am", I assert, as though all of my personality and demeanour were a given, not amenable to any modification by me. Asserting that I have no choice but to be who I am (and to behave in the ways I do), and that others must just "take me as they find me", makes my (lack of) freedom an issue for all who have to do with me. (And many of us know someone who "argues" in broadly these terms.)

There is something odd about this case from the beginning. Persons who say this are not *explaining* their behaviour, so much as justifying it. They assume it will stand in need of justification, in the sober light of day. But that cannot be a realistic stance for humanity as a group: we cannot all (and always) need excusing in these ways. To find that we always did so would be to undermine the distinctions between, roughly, the guilty and the innocent.

Notice, first, that this case does not turn on causal questions. Rather, it foregrounds responsibility: I am not free here because I am not responsible, whereas we might expect the inference to run in the opposite direction (Chapter 5, p. 76) – that I should not be held responsible because I am not free. Second, and perhaps for that reason, while this may be a question about free will, it is not mine. As I will urge (p. 148), the concern with what I can or cannot *change* is not the centre of the traditional problem of freedom of the will, at least, if (like me) that problem is one about causality. The third point connects this discussion with my others: it is that, far from opposing the possibility of action, this case presupposes it. Perhaps I am not free, but that point is only clear because (say) others are free; others such as repressive capitalists, or my teachers, etc. In any event, our philosophical response to this case parallels our practical one: to tell the person (a) to stop whining and (b) to get a grip on his or her life. Now, in some cases, this brisk reply will be misplaced: the person really is beset in numerous ways. But that example too makes the general point here, for, from the fact that this person is unable to act in ways the rest of us can, we are entitled to infer the obvious conclusion: the *general* possibility of agency. So, for this case too, there is no genuine issue unprovoked by philosophy.

The terms of the debate

The second relevant feature (noted above) identifying these concerns with free action as centrally *philosophical* is the way in which the key terms of this debate (in particular, "action", "reason", "cause", "necessity") are technical terms within philosophy. As has been recognized throughout this work, these terms are used in this debate as *terms of art* – even if they are making distinctions regularly drawn! The implication is of some reliable distinction here (some reliable use of the relevant term, as it were) to be contrasted with other distinctions that might be (or have been) drawn. So that, again, the robust procedures against scepticism of Dr Johnson (kicking a stone to prove the existence of the external world) or of G. E. Moore (exhibiting his hands to demonstrate the same idea: Moore 1959: 146) involve misunderstanding just because they treat the problems raised by sceptics in *other than* philosophical terms (Stroud 1984: 136).

However, we can "read" these cases quite differently, giving them a different moral: namely, that the terms of the debate are centrally those of philosophy; that taking those terms any other way produces a different set of issues, and ones that are soluble case-by-case.

In fact, this task would be facilitated not by calling the issue one concerned with *freedom of the will*, but rather with the possibility of genuine *actions*, of people doing things, while granting a world where the universal causation required for science is conceded. The contrast is not between my freely willed behaviour and my other kind, nor even between my willed behaviour and my other kinds; rather, it concerns whether or not there are agents. Suppose a guard is tortured into giving the combination to a nuclear weapons silo. Did this guard, "frightened, pained and bleeding" (Audi 1993: 186), give the combination freely? This highlights one of the problems for characterizing the issue in terms of *freedom* and/or *wills*. Like my "obedience" faced with a gunman [KEY CASE 3], what this guard did still constitutes an *action*, however circumscribed. Since this guard does something, (some) action is (sometimes) possible – that is my issue. And (again) the very generality of this issue highlights its philosophical pedigree: for lawyers, psychologists, etc., take at least their own action for granted.

Control

It might seem, though, that the resolution of the problem of free action sketched above leaves out something fundamental. For it has not given a sense of the expression "could have done otherwise", which explains how what humans *do* is causally explicable and also rationally motivated (or agency). Now it might be urged that this is central to any realistic free will defence: without it, in what sense do we have control of our "activities"?

This idea might be extracted from the account of personal autonomy sketched by Stephen Lukes, where actions are contrasted with situations where a person's behaviour is explained "[i] as an instrument or object of another's will or [ii] as a result of external or internal forces independent of his will" (1973: 101, *my numbers*). In this passage, we might think of Lukes as identifying both constraint at the level of action, in (i), and constraint at the level of causality, in (ii).

The response to this position has three elements. First, we must reiterate that our solution is sound; that the objections to the idea of agency came from the determinist argument (without that argument, we had no general ground for casting doubt on the possibility of agency). So those objections are indeed *met* once the argument is defused: nothing more is needed.

Second, the determinist need not advocate the "giant puppet-master" (Dennett 1984: 8–19; Fischer 1994: 17–19), whose plans or designs our lives follow. So one's control over behaviour as such is not really the determinist problem. Yet this is implicitly what is being appealed to in (i) above: the thought that one is being controlled by another. Rather, the determinist stresses the working out of causal laws, as might be suggested in (ii) above: falling bodies do not have *control*, the fall being explained by the working out of a natural law (say, gravitation). Of course, agency does in this way imply (the possibility of) control (of a sort); but the issue is the *possibility* of agency. If this possibility is granted, the question is just the practical one of what choices, or lack of them, I have in this case. That is, the topic becomes one concerning my practical control: is there some reason to suppose it is especially limited here (in contrast to the usual situation)?

Third, and relatedly, the expression "could have done otherwise" seems to get its force from the contrast with constraint: what we have is, effectively, the so-called *negative* account of freedom, where freedom is freedom from . . . well, constraint! (This is one insight of the "utilitarian" view, discussed in Chapter 5. Its reappearance here illustrates one part of the general strategy of this text: to pick up the insights behind the responses to determinism dismissed in previous chapters. For, although they are inadequate as responses, "there *is* good in them, poor things" (Wisdom 1953: 41, original emphasis).) And this is in line with our discussion of the kleptomaniac [KEY CASE 2]: that this person was not acting freely in *this* case, for just *that* reason. According to this view, then, I "couldn't have done X" if I was restrained from doing X in some way: I couldn't buy milk from the shop because (a) I had no money, or (b) the shop had sold out of milk, or (c) the shop did not sell milk (it was a newsagent), etc. In all these cases, I could not do a certain thing: the implication is that, without such constraints, I could have done so. (In the film *Destry Rides Again* (1939), the James Stewart character declines to give his guns to the villain: this is taken to mean that he *won't* do it whereas in reality he can't, as he is not wearing guns.) So, in line with the previous discussion of defeasibility (Chapter 8, p. 124), the thought is that I could have done other than I did unless . . ., where the "unless" is made concrete by citing the "head of exception" that applies in this case, with the burden of proof on the objector.

In elaboration, we should notice that an agent is acting freely if nothing at the level of actions restrains him (as in the case from Flew: Chapter 5, p. 73). This explains why a reductive account of the choice between two meals in a cafeteria is appropriate [KEY CASE 13](Chapter 6, p. 93); there is no constraint, so the action is free. It also illustrates why the sort of control of one's behaviour sought at the level of causality is not germane. As Ryle (1949: 66) noted, the question, "what makes a bodily movement voluntary?" was "wrongly supposed [to be] . . . a causal question": "wrongly" both because, given universal causality, this feature could not distinguish voluntary from involuntary and because concern with *control* (typically) addresses the extent of agency (or, sometimes, questions of psychological determinism, which were argued (Chapter 3) to turn on restrictions of agency too) but posed in a form of words that suggests (or can suggest) the determinist rejection of the possibility of action. If we then ask the question "To whom does it suggest this?", the answer is that given above: to philosophers.

One further issue concerning the idea of control relates to the difficulty of what account to give of what were called "desert concepts" (Chapter 6, p. 94): for the best that might be offered seemed to be a reductive account of choice, on which to choose is no more than to take the cheese salad in the cafeteria [KEY CASE 13]. But, as we noticed, that was insufficient to give weight to the kinds of responsibility for our actions that, as free will defenders, we have been keen to endorse. Or so it seemed.

Yet this is not quite right. First, what is being defended here is not just a *reductive* account of choice. On the contrary, the basis for thinking of choice as theoretically limited (as opposed to the practical limitations granted on all sides) has been the determinist argument With the rejection of that argument, we are simply thrown back on our own resources, to formulate accounts of choosing. A second thought is that, although we may not have good words to mark the contrasts, we do distinguish the kind of choosing that best fits the reductive account of choice from other kinds of choice: in particular, and revealingly, we think of the kinds of choosing that children, say, might do as not carrying the same moral weight as that of adults. We might well call the second of these, in different situations, "rational choice" or "considered choice": roughly, it is enshrined in law in terms of one's competence, such that children cannot sign legally binding documents, say, until they reach a certain age. A third thought grows from this one: that the choices we think of as our rational or considered choices (in the sense just noted) can still be ones explained after the fact; that the choice was not made on the basis of some piece of *prior planning* does not preclude its being explained by reference to wants, desires, intentions and the like. Indeed, this third point highlights one reason for detaching the discussion of *determinism* (as here) from that of *control*; namely, that the giving of rational explanation should not be equated with the hunting for prior planning, although both might be called "finding the reasons . . .".

Suppose someone with whom one has been having a conversation for some time broached the subject of control by asking, "If we travelled back five seconds, with everything else being the same, could you have said (or done) something different than you just did?". The "yes" answer has two parts. First, what, except for a theoretical commitment, would stop me accepting that. Clearly, no general consideration could (although one might not *want* to say the same), a thought reinforced by reflecting on the variety of things one considered saying, but chose not to. Second, the question is confusingly asked: since there is no finite totality of "everything else", the whole "thought experiment" really makes no sense.

So the absence of a sustained discussion of the idea of control was, as we have seen, a feature of the argument, rather than an omission from it. For the position on free action developed here does not involve giving a sense to the expression "could have done otherwise", but in urging (an insight noted in Chapter 5) that we already have such a sense based on our understanding of when behaviour is constrained.

And finally

This text has two over-arching aims, identified initially: to introduce (relative) beginners to philosophical problems concerning free action (or the freedom of the will) and to introduce those beginners to central ideas of philosophy. And, structurally, it was to do the second *through* doing the first. Such a structure was warranted partly because, since philosophy is an activity, being told about it is not a good way to come to understand it. Instead, one should watch philosophy being done (if in a self-conscious way) and begin doing it oneself. So, here, we have seen chains of argument and the insight (or illusion) from which they began; and we have countered them sometimes with considerations of their own internal consistency (in terms of their view of the issue) and sometimes by suggesting that other starting places are of equal value, or equal plausibility. And the considerations presented here have been reinforced through the identification of other, related issues that might be pursued.

In this vein, first, we have considered some (from among the many) responses to a determinist argument – although indicating ways in which these responses might be typical (at least, typical of species of argument). Equally, and second, I have offered a tentative dissolution of the problem as set up here. No doubt there is much more that a concerted determinist counter-blast could offer than has been considered here. These, then, are both ways that the arguments begun in this text could be taken further.

But there is another moral to be extracted, also suggestive of further work in philosophy. It would ask about assumptions taken for granted in this text: might not they too be seen from another perspective? Then, for instance, the history of philosophy might offer us models of alternative (to the ones assumed here) sets of conceptual connections. For example, in their writing on Descartes, Baker & Morris highlight (a) how knowledge of past philosophy "might lead us to a see an aspect of concepts to which we have been blind" (1996: 218) and (b) how "making a sustained effort to grasp Descartes' vision might lead us to a greater self-awareness" (*ibid.*: 219): it might lead to our coming to "read his texts with more humility" (*ibid.*: 219). This is surely appropriate for a major thinker, where the outcome might be "the possibility of recognizing conflicts of frameworks and responding to them intelligently" (*ibid.*: 219). In general, doing so might amount to changes in "nothing less than ways of seeing things or norms for describing them" (*ibid.*: 219). Recognizing that a plausible way to conceptualize a certain issue[8] is not the *only* way, and that gifted thinkers have conceptualized it differently, is not only a sobering thought, faced with the pretensions of contemporary views, but a basis for a re-thinking of our own position(s).

Appendix: chaos theory and determinism

One idea from (broadly) contemporary science which had captured both the attention of the media and (therefore?), to some degree, the general public is *chaos theory*, receiving a popular presentation in the novel *Jurassic Park* (Crichton 1991) and in the large-grossing film of the same title (1993). It presents a popular view that contemporary science is no longer deterministic in the way it had seemed in the past (and as I presented it here); the (assumed) conclusion that the world was somehow *chaotic* might seem to undermine the determinist's whole position, not least, by undermining the first premise of the argument (Chapter 2, p. 21).

As a preliminary, no substantial conclusion should be drawn from the name alone: do the assumptions and practices of chaos theory indeed suggest that the world is *chaotic*? As we will find, they do not! (The name "chaos theory" is just a name.)

There are two distinct (but related) threads within chaos theory. The first concerns its most famous thesis, the *butterfly effect*, or the thesis of "sensitive dependence on initial conditions" (Gleick 1987: 8). Suppose we wish to predict where a cannon-ball will fall to earth. If we genuinely knew the relevant causal laws (say, those relating to gravity, to air-resistance, to the mechanism of the cannon, and the like) and the relevant initial conditions (exact weight of the cannon ball, exact charge in the shell, exact wind conditions, etc.) we could predict exactly the cannon-ball's landing point. Of course, we typically do not know these things. We know at best some aspects of them, more and less exactly. Yet our linear assumptions are such that if we are *slightly* adrift in our knowledge of the initial conditions, etc., we shall be *slightly* off in our prediction: the cannon-ball will fall roughly where we predicted but not exactly. So far so good.

Chaos theorists accept that, for some physical systems, this assumption of linearity is warranted (or correct): for these systems, being slightly wrong about the initial conditions will result in the predictions also being slightly wrong. For such systems, of course, nothing new is being said.

A key discovery of chaos theory is that for some systems, those governed by non-linear equations, being slightly adrift in one's grasp of initial conditions can lead to being *hugely* wrong in one's predictions. One such non-linear system is the weather. Suppose a computer, programmed with the relevant causal laws, simulates the weather for the next few days. Slightly altering the initial conditions given to such a programme, and watching its weather predictions for the following few days, these slight variations in initial conditions can result in radically different outcomes. So the system is sensitive to the initial conditions, such that leaving out some tiny factor can result in hugely mistaken predictions. In the famous case, the difference in initial conditions caused by a butterfly flapping its wings in China could be, say, between there being or not being a hurricane in the USA. Hence the title: the butterfly effect.

This is a thesis about how our *knowledge* of initial conditions relates to the accuracy of our predictions. And it can make prediction hard. In the film *Jurassic Park*, the Laura Dern character guesses which way a drop of water, placed on the back of her hand, will run. It goes, say, towards the wrist. Now will a similar drop placed in the same spot run in the same direction? (Notice the simplicity of the problem: the water can only run towards wrist or towards finger-tips.) The initial conditions in these two "trials" are slightly different (partly because of the effects of the first water drop), so there is no "best guess" on the basis of the previous outcome. But if we knew all the initial conditions exactly, our predictions would be exact. The difficulty lies in knowing these conditions: especially in knowing them *all*. There is nothing genuinely *chaotic* here: indeed, the model is fully deterministic. The difficulty highlighted simply concerns human knowledge, and hence the (practical) difficulties of prediction. Further, the chaos theorist's preferred research tool is the computer. And a computer in a genuinely chaotic world, a chaotic computer, would be useless, since we could not rely on it! Finally, the emphasis on knowledge of outcomes and on the practicalities of predictions shows their irrelevance to our discussion of determinism: the determinist conceded the practical impossibility of prediction, and chaos theory grants predictability *in principle*.

The conclusion from this sketch of the butterfly effect is that nothing here need concern a determinist – if it offers no special comfort for him or her, equally it holds no special terrors.

The other thread in chaos theory is best introduced by reference to a paper by one of its founders, Benoit Mandelbrot: "How long is the coastline of Britain?" (see Gleick 1987: 94–6). Mandelbrot argues that this question has no answer. The coastline has no (determinate) length, because, for any answer, we can always find a (slightly) longer answer by looking into the yet finer structure of the coastline (say, some small indentation that we had not considered). Does this "expansion" have a limit? Mandelbrot's finding was that "as the scale of measurement becomes smaller, the measured length of a coastline rises without limit, bays and peninsulas revealing ever-smaller sub-bays and sub-peninsulas – at least down to atomic scales" (quoted in Gleick 1987: 96). Now, the "glossy" end of this thought is the idea of a fractal: a structure one can *always* look further into (*ibid.*: 98–9). And one of the most important ways of generating fractals on a computer was via a mathematical construction, the Mandelbrot set (*ibid.*: 221–32). This idea might be "applied" to the world around us, rather than the world of mathematics. For, if we cannot actually determine, say, the length of a coastline (where this is an "in principle" difficulty), then any predictions we made based on its length might seem problematic. These ideas might seem to generate (or explain) just the sort of "fuzziness" in the natural world incompatible with there being deterministic causal laws.

But, first, the vast complexity of structure does not prevent its being generated by a (deterministic) computer. Second, the right moral to draw from Mandelbrot's paper is this: ask a clear question, and you can get a clear answer! If we specify a certain smallest unit for our measurement of the coastline's length, implicitly ruling out some of the sub-bays or sub-peninsulas, we will get a final answer. So, far from suggesting that *no* answer is possible here, the conclusion from chaos theory is that no *final* answer is possible. But this is a comment on the incoherence of the idea of a *final answer* (because we cannot ask a final question!) and a justification for being content with the answer to the question that was asked. Third, this is a thesis about *all* the objects in the world. So, finding that it precluded causal laws would preclude them for tables, chairs and the like, as well as for agents. Or, if it did not preclude them, there would still be causal laws, with causal necessity (and hence determinism). There is no special hope that this view of sciencen(this "new science", as Gleick calls it) offers a different reading of the evidential base for the first premise of the determinist argument than that offered by other conceptions of science.

Notes

Chapter 1 – Free will: the issue

1. In fact, modern discussions of *willing* (compare Kane (1996: 22–31)), such as those raised in Chapter 7, just highlight the centrality of action.

2. Also called "corn circles": one group studying this phenomenon was called "The Centre for Corn Circle Studies".

3. An obvious and important omission here (and throughout) is the case of animals: are they agents? Well, certainly it is more tempting to take the gorilla as an agent than, say, the limpet – limpet-behaviour seems explicable via the sorts of chemical processes used to explain plants "turning" towards the light. Here I simply put aside animal cases until we have a better grip on the human situation, which takes us beyond this text!

4. There are many important complexities around the notions of the intentional, the voluntary and the deliberate (as well as the accidental and the inadvertent: for a sophisticated discussion, see Austin (1970: 175–204, 185 n.1)). Here, I am sketching a contrast (or set of contrasts) in the broadest terms, to be refined through later discussion.

5. The term is sometimes misused for shoplifting, but I am not considering that case here. Ayer (1954: 280) is among the philosophers using a contrast between thief and kleptomaniac similar to mine.

6. My thanks to the reader whose remarks on the phenomenology of belching aided me here.

7. Again, I am here putting aside both the case of animals and of children responding to the direction of adults, although later remarks might suggest a line here.

8. Much contemporary philosophy takes for granted that it is *events* that cause *events*: that is, that both cause and effect are events. Thus, an introductory text begins its account of causation: "if an event of the first kind occurs, an event of the second kind will or must occur, and the first event will explain the occurrence of the second event" (Bunnin and Tsui-James 1996: 744).

For this reason, this assumption is made here. As we will note, the idea of a causal chain is facilitated by conceiving of all the "links" in the chain as events, since they then seem to be "all the same type of thing".
9. This should be regarded as a technical use of the term "determinism", which does not line up with all other uses of it.
10. It is important to remind ourselves that there are other kinds of predictability: as F. H. Bradley asks rhetorically: "What sayings in life are more common than, 'You might have known me better. I never could have done such a thing,' or 'It was impossible for me to act so, and you ought to have known that nothing could have made me'?" (1962: 13).

Bradley's point (and surely one well taken) is that we expect a *certain* kind of predictability of human behaviour, which is why I can be justifiably concerned that you fail to predict my behaviour, as instanced in the expressions he quotes. So the objection is not to predictability *as such* but to a certain type of predictability. (My thanks to Katherine Morris for bringing this to my attention; and for reminding me of the passage from Bradley.)
11. See, for instance, Carruthers (1986: esp. 49–51) and Kenny (1992a: esp. Chs 2, 3, 5).
12. The expression "to beg the question" has deteriorated in common speech until it has become virtually equivalent to "to invite the question". Here I use the expression in its technical sense, meaning "to build-in the answer" to one's question in the formulation of that question.

Chapter 2 – Determinism: exposition

1. The literature includes soft and hard determinists, and economic, psychological or biological determinists. The safest view for the beginner is, first, to stick with just one set of cases to call *determinism* oneself (I suggest the one used here) then, second, to consider how any author uses the term, often best done by seeing what determinism is *contrasted* with. For instance, if "psychological determinism" were contrasted with the idea of unlimited choice, it would just be the plausible and harmless idea (from Chapter 1) that what one can choose depends on one's previous choices and on the circumstances – nothing determinist (in our sense) in that! Philosophical discussions are often rendered difficult both by the same term being used in different contexts, and by the idiocy of some of the titles that positions have ended up with. The only hope is to be clear what contrasts one is drawing.
2. I take the usual option, "hard determinist", to have a strong potential to confuse the beginner, since other kinds (for example, soft determinists) do not reach the same conclusion: as this is a species of free will defence (see Chapter 6), it is neater to think of it as no kind of determinism!
3. This was not, say, an assumption of (some) alchemical writing, where the very same ingredients in the same proportions were thought to possibly have different outcomes. Here too (p. 24), the issue of causal continuity assumes "same cause, same effect" and "different effect, different cause", as alchemy did not.

4. Complications here might arise from interpretations of, say, the uncertainty principle from modern physics: for discussion, see Chapter 4, pp. 59–62.

5. I consider another reading of Dennett's point in Chapter 8.

6. In this way, it runs together what Honderich (1993: 3) insists are two separate questions, about our nature and about its implications. But there is no philosophical thesis in a claim about our nature solely: to get a philosophical thesis we must ask what implications these "facts" about our nature have.

7. O'Connor (1971: 12) urges that (in his version at least) it is a valid argument!

8. Nagel (1979: 181–95) has argued that, although panpsychism (the doctrine that all the basic constituents have mental properties) is a crazy view, it is no more crazy than any of the standard competitor views: but, in respect of free will, ascribing freedom to the inanimate seems to go beyond any plausibility.

9. In this context this expression sometimes means simply adherence to the first premise of the determinist argument, that all events have causes. But it can also mean (as here) that the causes themselves are those described by the physical sciences.

10. In this vein, Williams writes of science providing an "absolute conception of the world" (1985: 139). For discussion, see Putnam (1992: Ch. 5).

11. This expression, from David Hume's "Abstract" to his *A Treatise of Human Nature* (1978 [1740]: 662), was used by J. L. Mackie (1974) as the title of a book on causality.

12. Named for the eighteenth-century Scots philosopher, David Hume: to avoid scholarly questions, simply treat it as an interesting view widely ascribed to Hume. See Danto (1989: 257–64) and G. Strawson (1989: 84–93, 145–73).

13. Some, for example Kenny (1968: esp. 216–26), have thought this an insoluable problem for the French philosopher René Descartes, who (it is often thought) took body and minds to share no properties in common.

14. For the imputation to Freud, consider Salmon (1974: esp. 272–5) and Flew & Vesey (1987: 61). For Marx, see Berlin (1939).

Chapter 3 – Determinism: qualifications and clarifications

1. To understand *dilemmas*, see Shaw (1981: 56–8).

2. There is an assumption here (see also Chapter 1, p. 4) that causes are themselves events, the outcome of prior causes: there is a long tradition in which this view is denied (see, for instance, Charlton (1990: 98–123)). Here, though, I assume that view, as I think a concerted determinist must.

3. As Nagel recognises: "Since the class of known physical properties is constantly expanding, the physical cannot be defined in terms of the concepts of contemporary physics, but must be more general" (1979: 183). Still, this gives the right idea.

4. As suggested above, first, any such account must treat causes here in the manner of causes elsewhere: so that if there were, say, necessarily causal laws elsewhere, the term 'cause' should here also imply causal laws, etc.; second, the most plausible case for determinism should be made. I think this is in terms from natural science. If so, it is not obvious where this would leave those who accept, say, psychological causes. Clearly the idea of "agent causation" (see p. 40) cannot be what such theorists intend.

5. One alternative: to think that determinism is undermined since behaviour is related to "state of information" (Popper 1957: 13; Trusted 1984: 87; Flew & Vesey 1987: 77; Sappington 1990). The idea of *information* is elaborated in the work of Donald M. MacKay, applied to free will in MacKay (1967), which, despite its title, defends a species of libertarianism (see Chapter 4). This argument may therefore be his: Dennett (1984: 61n) says so.

6. See Flew for a relevant example:

> consider . . . my hearing the news that some favoured enemy has suffered a misfortune. I may choose to construe this as a cause for celebration. If I do, then it will be correct both for me and for everybody else to say that my hearing of this news was both my reason for celebrating and the cause of my celebration. Nevertheless, I was an agent in the whole business, not a patient. Nothing and no one compelled me to celebrate, to make whoopee willy nilly. I could instead – and, had I been a nicer person, perhaps I would – have taken the acquisition of exactly the same information as a cause for commiseration. (Flew & Vesey 1987: 56)

Here a free will defender accepts the sense in which I "could not do otherwise", but without becoming a determinist.

Chapter 4 – Libertarianism: two varieties

1. A section of one of Campbell's most important papers is in Berofsky (1966); the fullest exposition is Campbell (1967).

2. Campbell (1967: 46–7) says that the only situation to be considered is one in which what the agent wants to do "is believed by him to be incompatible with what is right".

3. Campbell tends to treat these inclinations as flowing from one's character (for example, Campbell (1967: 46)).

4. For example, he speaks of the "line of least resistance" (Campbell 1967: 49) in following one's inclinations.

5. See, for example, Campbell on the importance of:

> being able to apprehend operations from the inside, from the stand point of living experience. But if we adopt this internal standpoint . . . the situation is entirely changed. We find that we not merely can, but constantly do, attach meaning to a causation which is the self's causation. (1967: 48)

Those who fail to do this, Campbell thinks, "restrict themselves . . . to an inadequate standpoint" (1967: 49).

6. Although arguably Campbell's use of the contrast is not Kant's, this distinction originates in the philosophy of Kant: classically in his *Groundwork of the Metaphysics of Moral* (1948: esp. 63–5). The beginner might start with Scruton (1982: 65–85), and then consider Guyer (1993: 335–93).

7. This is not to speak against the distinction as such (say, in Kant's use: see earlier note) but against its being indicative of the contrast between the causal ("from inclination") and the non-causal ("from duty").

8. Compare Campbell on Heisenberg etc.: "I am not myself . . . disposed to rest any part of the case against universal determinism upon these recent dramatic developments of physical science" (1967: 45).

9. See Scruton: "The fundamental laws of the universe do not enable us to deduce the future from the past. They only say that certain events are probable, given certain others" (1994: 227–8). Any other view is dismissed as "a very old-fashioned view of science" (Scruton 1996: 98). But compare Honderich (1993: 62 ff.).

Chapter 5 – Compatibilism I: the "utilitarian" position

1. The variety of compatibilism should be noted. The structure here (and in Chapter 6) is to offer a map into which other variants might be fitted; and where the response from this view should be fairly clear. For example, is conceding universal causation at the level of the physical combated by finding a different kind of explanatory framework (than the physical) for actions, say, as intentional behaviour characterized in terms of antecedent psychological states? (Answering "yes" suggests some kind of "two-language" view.) If so, are the psychological states thought of causally? (Answering "yes" narrows the field, as not all theorists do take the intentional as causal: see Melden 1961; Kenny 1992a: 144–5.) And are there covering laws for such causes? See Chapter 6, note 4.

2. See Quinton (1973) for a good (and fairly elementary) general account; and Williams (1972: 96–112) for a clear critical discussion.

3. Among others, see Ayer (1954) and Schlick (1966). Berofsky (1966: 294) also attributes this position to Nowell-Smith.

4. Thus Ayer (whose position had changed) still asked, "What are the limitations upon the agent's freedom?" (1984: 10); and responded, "The emphasis falls on the denial of freedom" (1984: 12).

5. In making this explicit connection to ideas of punishment, Schlick is reiterating ideas from J. S. Mill (quoted and discussed by Trusted (1984: 42–3)). (Since Mill was a major theorist of utilitarian moral philosophy, this is another justification of my title for this position.)

6. Van Inwagen is here giving an exposition of a view he rejects; and goes on to argue against.

7. This is a species of paradigm case argument: see Passmore (1961: 100–18) and Flew (1956: 1–20).

8. To follow up this point, see the writings of J. L. Austin (1970: esp. 175–204, 253–71, 272–87). The fact that Austin typically wrote limpid sentences can obscure the complexity of his thought.
9. This might put pressure on the claim that the kleptomaniac is not really free. But the utilitarian articulates his free/constrained contrast with cases like this: finding that this was not, after all, a case of *constraint* would weaken his position (at least, if it applied to all or most of his preferred cases of constraint, and why should it not?). Equally, this is a case where the free will defender's intuitions coincide with those of his opponent.
10. The most common such "measure" is given in the slogan: "the greatest happiness of the greatest number"(see Quinton 1973: 1–10).

Chapter 6 – Compatibilism II: the two-language view

1. On the relation of soft determinist to compatibilism, see Thornton (1989: esp. 133–4).
2. See Thornton (1989: 41, 44) for a set of uses resembling mine, although different from it.
3. The term "language" is in scare-quote marks here because these are not really languages at all, but merely segments of ways of explaining.
4. Reference to some other versions of compatibilism appear in the "Extended and annotated reading". Often the differences can be related to the discussion here. For instance, as we will see, Davidson (at least in most modes) is a two-language theorist since, for him, bodily description is precisely not connected to action-description in the way other causal descriptions might be conjoined: one cannot (in principle) write laws for the kinds of psychological phenomena that are appealed to in explaining actions: "there are no strict laws that cover events or states described in psychological terms" (Davidson 1980: xv).

    For Davidson, there *are* such laws in natural science: so psychological explanation, although causal, is nevertheless anomalous when compared with explanation in science (since it lacks laws: "no law lurks" (*ibid.*: 53)). So the sorts of "mental events" used in action-explanations "resist capture in the nomological net of physical theory" (*ibid.*: 207).

    But why exactly is that? As he reports it, "there may be true general statements relating the mental and the physical . . . but they are not lawlike" (*ibid.*: 216). Yet how is this lack of "law-likeness" explained? If there are laws (of natural science) connecting bodily movements in such a way as to permit causal description, how can we deny that there are laws for the actions thereby performed?

    Davidson's argument here has two parts: first, there is a thesis about action-description, such that "causal relations . . . hold between events however described" (*ibid.*: 243). So, for him, there are not two events here, nor two causes. But the second thesis relates those event-descriptions to laws (or law-likenesses): "if *a* caused *b*, then some descriptions of *a* and *b* instantiate a strict causal law. But the law is never . . . a psychophysical law, nor can it be purely psychological . . ." (*ibid.*: 243)

Here, it is their statistical nature that precludes genuinely psychological laws. Notice the contrast between the psychological law, relating the psychological with the psychological (see Chapter 3), and the psychophysical law, relating the bodily and the psychological: in denying the second, Davidson is offering a version of "two-language" view, in which action descriptions are not translatable to those law-like event-descriptions beloved of natural science.

5. Events may be describable in either way (see below) but conceptualizing the event one way precludes conceptualizing it the other way in the same breath: or so the position asserts.

6. One might demoralize the bowling and break the pavilion clock and hit the biggest six on that cricket ground and win the county championship, but there would be just *one* causal story of bat, ball, clockface, and so on: see Best (1974: 39).

7. On *entailment*, and other logical notions, see Shaw (1981: esp. Ch. 3).

8. Note that, while these all purport to be causal, they are not all at the level of causation, the micro-level, espoused earlier.

9. This is substitution of expressions "preserving truth", *salva veritate*, so that if the statement was true before it must be true now; and if not, not.

10. The word derives from the Greek for *end* or *purpose*: see Taylor (1964: 5–6); Trusted (1984: 30–31); Kenny (1992b: 79–85). An amusing example (if gruesome, and North American) of powerfully teleological "thinking" is provided by Haugeland (1998: 144).

11. If we attribute agency here to God, that is precisely to treat the matter no longer entirely causally.

12. See Honderich (1988b: 69–70), where he discusses a "principle of desert". Honderich also, and rightly, emphasizes that there may be a problem for "compatibilists"; that is, the two-language view here (Honderich 1988b: 177).

13. Ginet (1990: 93 n.2) cites important work by Frankfurt (1969) to suggest that there may be moral responsibility without choice: see Fischer (1994: 131–59) for discussion (Ginet cites an earlier discussion by Fischer); also Chapter 7.

Chapter 7 – The irrelevance of determinism?

1. Similar objections have been raised against Strawson's assumption of: "a massive core of human thinking that has no history – or none recorded in histories of thought; there are concepts and categories which, in their most fundamental character, change not at all" (Strawson 1959: 10). Similarly, Strawson's (Kantian?) methods here resemble those under discussion.

2. This discussion touches only one aspect of Strawson's (complex) position; and that indirectly. Some ideas for a fuller response are in "A guide to further reading".

3. Interestingly, Fischer's own version differs from mine: on his version (translated into my case), Green's intervention is simply to compel Grey to

want to vote Conservative (Fischer 1994: 131–4). This revision makes the case even more obviously to do with agent-psychology; from the perspective of *this* text, that seems to weaken it.
4. Frankfurt might explain this by conceding that Grey lacks the appropriate "second-order volitions" (Watson 1982: 86): See Thornton (1989: 112–14) and Ginet (1990: 120).

Chapter 8 – The very idea of causal necessity

1. Hampshire (1989: 83); the discussion here owes a lot to Hampshire, especially this work.
2. Wilkerson (1974: 162); McFee (1992: 64).
3. Compare Jeans (discussed and quoted in Stebbing 1937: 47–54).
4. Contrast Bernard Williams's picture of a "world as it is independent of our experience", the root of his absolute conception (Williams 1985: 139) of the world; Williams is committed to the finality of such a description. As Putnam (1992: 83) states it, for Williams "the world we live in, the world with observers, evolved out of the world without observers. So a description . . . that we need to describe the world without observers must be possible".

  Is this line of thinking as persuasive as it at first appears? As Putnam continues:

  > it is true that with the evolution of animals and human beings . . . no new physical laws came into existence . . . [but] With the appearance of living things and societies new laws do appear; not laws which contradict the laws of physics, but laws which are not available in physics . . . the question of "explaining the relation between supply and demand" is not a meaningful question to address to a physicist.   (1992: 83)

  As Putnam notes, the issues raised by the economist, say, are not automatically "translatable" into issues for the physicist. We could also point out the unreliability, even within causal descriptions, of the kind of "inter-translatability" rejected: even when one form of words is available, that does not guarantee that only one question is being addressed!
5. Of course, this generates a false isolation (Hampshire 1989: 83): the need to exclude counter-possibilities involves withdrawing typical assumptions of constancy (at least defeasibly: see p. 124).
6. See Travis (1981: 143–55).
7. See, for example, the discussion of laws in Malthus (1970: 32), from which these examples are taken.
8. Perhaps the topic of another book!
9. My special thanks to Bob Brecher for discussion of this topic.
10. See, for instance, Robinson:

  > Without the possibility of controlled experiment, we have to rely on the interpretation of evidence . . .   (1962: 26)

      . . . economics limps along with one foot in untested hypotheses and
      the other in untestable slogans.   (1962: 28)

11. See, too, Dennett (1998: 305–6) on experiments (on Vervet monkey) that
    can only be done once!
12. The same point applies to statistical generalizations: if we assert that *X* will
    occur 60% of the time, this too will not be exceptionless; we cannot
    assume that the sixty-first percentile will be non-*X*!

Chapter 9 – Conclusions and reflections on philosophical method

1. "Trend"/"tendency" data are indicative of correlation, not causality; yes,
    but (given some explanatory addition) it might represent the (broadly)
    causal . . .
2. Compare Davidson: "psychological generalisations must be irreducibly
    statistical in character, in contrast to sciences" (1980: 240).
3. George Berkeley, *Philosophical Commentaries* §405: "side with the vulgar
    against the learned". Also his *Three Dialogues between Hylas and
    Philonous* (in Berkeley 1910: 200), turning from the views of the learned
    to "vulgar opinions".
4. See also Baker (1992: 115–16, 127–31). Wittgenstein's position on the
    freedom of the will, to judge by notes by Yorick Smythies (Wittgenstein
    1993) from two lectures (probably delivered in 1939), resembled that
    advocated here: contrast Dilman (1999: 234–54).
5. In fact, the case was complicated by, first, the judge distinguishing a legal
    responsibility for the crime from a moral responsibility: the confessions
    were taken to guarantee legal responsibility, so that only the moral respon-
    sibility was at issue. Second, and relatedly, the argument was only in
    mitigation of their behaviour: there was no suggestion that they might be
    wholly blameless. As a result of the defence "Leopold and Loeb escaped
    execution and were sentenced to life imprisonment" (Cahn 1972: 76).
6. In particular, I am aware how badly this fits Hinduism: for some relevant
    discussion, see Danto (1972: 28–32).
7. My thanks to Katherine Morris, for suggesting this case in conversation.
8. Note here the dubious assumption that there is one issue, once we agree
    that there are two accounts.

A guide to further reading

In addition to commenting on some texts used throughout (or in particular chapters in) this work, this reading list mentions and annotates texts with very different conceptions of the whole topic. The selection here is based on my wanting (with reservations noted) to *recommend* these books, as ways of augmenting the argument of this text.

As the body of the text suggests, O'Connor (1971), Trusted (1984) and Thornton (1989) are excellent brief introductions. Each has its virtues, with Thornton providing a very useful map by sketching many of the most widely adopted positions and possibilities, and incorporating a useful bibliography. Pears (1963) is a collection of discussions by major philosophers, now slightly dated, but likely to generate enthusiasm for central questions. Young (1991) highlights something of the philosophical centrality of the issue, briefly, and in rather the way it is conceived here. In addition, Charlton (1990: Chs 6 & 7) and Scruton (1994: Ch. 17) locate, respectively, the nature of change and the philosophy of action in a clear way in more general philosophical concerns. Dilman (1999), a difficult text, offers revealing discussion of the relation of key theorists from the past of philosophy (and elsewhere) to the freedom of action.

Conceptions of the nature of persons (and especially the question of how their physical character relates to their psychological powers and capacities) are usefully discussed, in an introductory way, in McGinn (1999: Ch. 1), and in more complex versions in Pettit (1993), as well as Wilkerson (1974). As the body of the text makes plain, various other conceptions of causality might usefully be assayed: Mackie (1974) remains a classic discussion here, while Charlton (1990: Ch. 6) both highlights some difficulties with Mackie's view and explores some other possibilities, as does Strawson (1989: 231–61). Mellor (1995) is a difficult but powerful study with a strong bibliography.

There are many useful anthologies on the free will problem, too many to cite without favouritism. My favourites are used in the body of the text: Berofsky (1966), which contains some classic sources; White (1968), a collection of major texts on the nature of action; Watson (1982), which, in addition to containing an excellent overview essay together with a useful bibliography, brings together some more recent sources. Many of the challenges these volumes identify have not yet been met. Other excellent anthologies, especially of more modern writing, are found in the bibliographies of texts discussed below; but much recent writing has been book-length.

While this text attempts to follow-through one line of argument, concerning free action, it is recognized that there are other versions both of the issues and of possible lines of solution. Although the keen student could probably reconstruct these from the text, I will consider some of the central categories identified in the text, in order to highlight some features of some key (recent-ish) work. (Most are considerably more difficult than this text.)

First, three contemporary varieties of libertarianism.
1. Van Inwagen (1983) presents a sustained discussion of a key aspect of the problem in a lively style. He argues for a species of incompatibilism, by taking a strong view on the inescapability of laws. Having reviewed traditional arguments, including the cases of alternate possibilities drawn from Frankfurt (1969)(see my Chapter 7), he concludes that moral responsibility requires freedom in a sense incompatible with the determinist thesis that universal causation leads to one unique future. As long as our argument for moral responsibility is stronger than our argument for such determinism, we should therefore accept the freedom of action. He concludes both that the argument here *is* stronger, and that it is the only argument for free will that one might have. He includes powerful

discussions of "could have done otherwise". (This is probably the recent book from which I have benefited most greatly, even where I differ from it.)

2. Although only a couple of his papers address the issue of free action, the line developed in Wiggins (1987) has been influential; and rightly so. It assumes that the threat of determinism has disappeared when discoveries in modern physics rethink the notion of causation; and therefore is directed primarily at the nature of *practical reason* (thereby displaying its Aristotelian heritage), and questions the precise relation of free action to belief and knowledge. Wiggins regards as crucial the need for a reliable account of libertarianism, since he finds it as problematic as a reliable account of compatibilism.

3. Kane (1996) offers an account of free will that is initially explained in terms of the agent as initiator. At the heart of Kane's own view is his commitment to its being the will that is at issue. He urges that one must address the compatibility of free will with universal causation, and ask why we might find "wantable" a free will incompatible with such causation. Taken together, he calls these "the Ascent problem" since, if their answers suggest a plausible incompatibilist account (as Kane concludes they do), we need still to address "the Descent problem": whether such an account of freedom is actually coherent or intelligible; and, if it is, does it actually exist "in the natural order" (Kane 1996: 13). Further, he argues that previous discussions have failed to take incompatibilism seriously enough because they have failed to see the Ascent problem as depending on the Descent one: once the coherence of the conception is granted, the intelligibility of incompatibilist freedom serves to work against such hasty dismissals. In managing the Ascent question, Kane considers the Frankfurt-type cases of alternative possibilities, contrasting his view with that of Fischer (see below) as well as van Inwagen. In discussing the Descent problem, we rehearse ideas from Wiggins and Honderich (see below).

This book is difficult both in content and style: its plethora of numbered theses, often closely related while different, make it hard to keep all of the argument in one's head at any one time. A book for the serious student only.

Second, three, or perhaps five, (different-ish) compatibilists.

4. Davidson is a key theorist here, especially for many compatibilists: many of his key papers are collected in Davidson (1980), but he has not addressed the issue at book-length (see Chapter 6, note 4 for some elaboration). Davidson takes compatibilism to be ensured (via various theses in the philosophy of language) because the description of events as actions resists codification into laws (or the lawlike) in ways description as (physical) events does not. Hence, although reasons functional causally, there can be no psychophysical laws. In this sense, the questions raised for the "two-language" view will represent issues that Davidson's position must address. For if there is a causal law determining the movements of a body (a physical law), the sense in which one's actions are none the less free may remain obscure – the absence of a psychophysical law need not deter our determinist.

5. Audi (1993), like Wiggins, is primarily concerned with the understanding of *practical reasoning*: he distinguishes four problems, only one of which really concerns the nature of free action. But his general background treats the explanation of action as at once causal and dependent on psychological states ("intentionalistic grounds of action")(*ibid.*: 4) rather than physical ones; and he gives considerable attention to arguing that the "logical" connection of reason to (its) action does not preclude causal connection.

6. Fischer (1994) disputes van Inwagen's view of the inescapability of laws, and thus defends a different conception of laws of nature, based on distinguishing two senses of "render false". From the beginning, central issues for Fischer turn on the role of *control* and *alternative possibilities* in regard to moral responsibility (although the need to say more about ourselves as practical reasoners is acknowledged (1994: 206). Like van Inwagen, Fischer gives considerable attention to the Frankfurt-type cases; and also considers briefly Frankfurt's discussion of "second-order volitions" (see Thornton (1989: 112–14) for a simple account) as offering at least some cases sufficient for free will. He develops a view, sometimes called "semicompatibilism", in which moral responsibility is compatible with determinism because moral responsibility does not require that

the agent "could have done otherwise" (although the agent being able to do otherwise is not, in the same way, compatible). And, of course, if causality were incompatible with "could have done otherwise", this thesis would be equally powerful – offering material for a coherent incompatibilism!

7. Although officially an opponent of both compatibilism and incompatibilism, offering "a refutation of both these traditional views" (Honderich 1988b: 119), Honderich (1988a,b) is actually a kind of compatibilist, since the true belief in determinism is compatible with notions of choice applying – it is (roughly) a matter of "level". Although calling himself a *determinist*, Honderich stresses the idea (shared with this text) that "universal causation" implied by the project of modern science does not preclude freedom of action: indeed, the language of presentation includes "psychoneural pairs". This is not a work for the faint-hearted. Honderich has written his own "summary" of central theses of his work (Honderich 1993), although this may strike many readers, as it strikes Honderich (*ibid.*: 5), as *hurried*.

8. Dennett (1984) is a vigorous presentation of a kind of compatibilism. The energy of the writing is not always translatable into clear argumentation, but its collection of "intuition pumps", Bugbears, Nefarious Neurosurgeons, and the wantability of free will (in some varieties) make it a charming and appealing contribution to the rhetoric of free will. This is a tremendously successful set of lectures, always thought-provoking, with a developed commitment to the idea of free action from a perspective that begins from the author's rationality (*ibid.*: 155).

Two other problems?

9. Lucas (1989) describes a quite different kind of problem, centrally concerned with the relationships between freedom and foreknowledge. Although presented in a form aided by some familiarity with presentation in logic, it does not (as some of Lucas's other work does) in general actually *require* them, except in two key passages on modal logic. This is a challenging but rewarding text, by a skilful writer.

10. P. Strawson (1974: 1–25) is an influential paper (widely reprinted), that does not get a fair hearing in this text. As

indicated, it is primarily concerned with the feelings, attitudes and reactions of persons as a way to "defend" a core feature of compatibilism by reference to the inevitability of our commitments to those attitudes, practices, etc. A sympathetic brief account, highlighting difficulties but emphasizing insights, is G. Strawson (1986: Ch. 5).

Bibliography

Audi, R. 1993. *Action, Intention, Reason*. Ithaca, NY: Cornell University Press.

Austin, J. L. 1970. *Philosophical Papers*, 2nd edn. Oxford: Clarendon Press.

Ayer, A. J. 1954. *Philosophical Essay*. London: Macmillan.

Ayer, A. J. 1963. *The Concept of a Person, and other Essays*. London: Macmillan.

Ayer, A. J. 1984. *Freedom and Morality, and other Essays*. Oxford: Oxford University Press.

Baker, G. 1977. Defeasibility and meaning. In *Law, Morality and Society*, P. Hacker & J. Raz (eds), 26–57. Oxford: Clarendon Press.

Baker, G. 1992. Some remarks on "language" and "grammar". *Grazer Philosophische Studien* **42**, 107–31.

Baker, G. and P. Hacker 1980. *Wittgenstein: Understanding and Meaning (Volume One of A Commentary on* Philosophical Investigations*)*. Oxford: Blackwell.

Baker, G. and K. Morris 1996. *Descartes' Dualism*. London: Routledge.

Berkeley, G. 1910. *A New Theory of Vision and other Writings*. London: Everyman.

Berlin, I. 1939. *Karl Marx: His Life and Environment*. London: Thornton Publishing.

Berofsky, B. (ed.) 1966. *Free Will and Determinism*. New York: Harper & Row.

Best, D. 1974. *Expression in Movement and the Arts*. London: Henry Kimpton.

Best, D. 1978. *Philosophy and Human Movement*. London: Allen and Unwin.

Bird, A. 1998. *Philosophy of Science*. London: UCL Press.

Bradley, F. H. 1962 [1876]. *Ethical Studies*, 2nd edn. Oxford: Oxford University Press (originally published in 1876, London: H. S. King & Co).

Bradley, F. H. 1969 [1893]. *Appearance and Reality*, 2nd edn. Oxford: Oxford University Press (originally published in 1893, London: Swan Sonneschein & Co.).

Bunnin, N. & E. P. Tsui-James (eds) 1996. *The Blackwell Companion to Philosophy*. Oxford: Blackwell.

Cahn, S. 1972. Does man have free will? In *Philosophical Issues: A Contemporary Introduction*, J. Rachels & F. Tillman (eds), 75–87. New York: Harper & Row.

Campbell, C. A. 1967. *In Defence of Free Will*. London: Allen and Unwin.

Carruthers, P. 1986. *Introducing Persons*. London: Croom Helm.

Carruthers, P. 1992. *Human Knowledge and Human Nature*. Oxford: Oxford University Press.

Chalmers, A. F. 1999. *What is this Thing Called Science?* 3rd edn. Buckingham: Open University Press.

Charlton, W. 1990. *The Analytic Ambition*. Oxford: Blackwell.

Crichton, M. 1991. *Jurassic Park*. London: Random Century Group.

Dancy, J. 1993. *Moral Reasons*. Oxford: Blackwell.

Danto, A. 1972. *Mysticism and Morality*. Harmondsworth: Penguin.

Danto, A. 1989. *Connections to the World*. New York: Harper & Row.

Darrow, C. 1957. *Attorney for the Damned*, A. Weinberg (ed.). New York: Simon and Schuster.

Davidson, D. 1980. *Essays on Actions and Events*. Oxford: Clarendon Press.

Dennett, D. 1984. *Elbow Room; the Varieties of Free Will Worth Wanting*. Oxford: Oxford University Press.

Dennett, D. 1991. *Consciousness Explained*. London: Allen Lane.

Dennett, D. 1998. *Brainchildren: Essays on Designing Mind*. Cambridge, MA: MIT/Bradford Books.

Descartes, R. 1984 [1641]. *The Philosophical Writings of Descartes*, Volume II, J. Cottingham, R. Stoothoff, D. Murdoch (trans.). Cambridge: Cambridge University Press (originally published 1641).

Dilman, I. 1975. *Matter and Mind*. London: Macmillan.

Dilman, I. 1984. *Freud and the Mind*. Oxford: Blackwell.

Dilman, I. 1999. *Freewill: An Historical and Philosophical Introduction*. London: Routledge.

Doyal, L. & R. Harris 1986. *Empiricism, Explanation and Rationality: An Introduction to the Philosophy of the Social Sciences*. London: Routledge.

Feynman, R. 1992 [1965]. *The Character of Physical Law*. Harmondsworth: Penguin.

Fischer, J. M. 1994. *The Metaphysics of Free Will*. Oxford: Blackwell.

Flew, A. 1956. Philosophy and language. In *Essays in Conceptual Analysis*, A. Flew (ed.), 1–20. London: Macmillan.

Flew, A. 1973. *Crime or Disease?* London: Macmillan.

Flew, A. 1986. Apologia pro philosophia mea. In *Philosophy in Britain Today*, S. Shanker (ed.), 72–97. London: Croom Helm.

Flew, A. and G. Vesey 1987. *Agency and Necessity*. Oxford: Blackwell.

Frankfurt, H. 1969. Moral responsibility and alternative possibilities. *Journal of Philosophy* 66: 829–39.

Frankfurt, H. 1992 [1971]. Freedom of the will and the concept of a person. In *Free Will*, G. Watson (ed.), 81–95. Oxford: Oxford University Press.

Frege, G. 1960. On concept and object. In *Philosophical Writings of Gottlob Frege*, P. Geach & M. Black (eds), 42–55. Oxford: Blackwell.

Gamow, G. 1962. *Biography of Physics*. London: Hutchinson.

Ginet, C. 1990. *On Action*. Cambridge: Cambridge University Press.

Gleick, J. 1987. *Chaos: Making a New Science*. London: Sphere Books.

Guyer, P. 1993. *Kant and the Experience of Freedom*. Cambridge: Cambridge University Press.

Hampshire, S. 1982 [1959]. *Thought and Action*. London: Chatto & Windus.

Hampshire, S. 1989. *Innocence and Experience*. Harmondsworth: Penguin.

Haugeland, J. 1998. *Having Thought: Essays in the Metaphysics of Mind*. Cambridge, MA: Harvard University Press.

Hobson, A. 1988. Psychoanalytic dream theory: a critique based on modern neurophysiology. In *Mind, Psychoanalysis and Science*, P. Clark & C. Wright (eds), 277–308. Oxford: Blackwell.

Honderich, T. 1988a. *Mind and Brain*, volume 1 of *A Theory of Determinism*. Oxford: Clarendon.

Honderich, T. 1988b. *The Consequences of Determinism*, volume 2 of *A Theory of Determinism*. Oxford: Clarendon.

Honderich, T. 1993. *How Free are You?* Oxford: Oxford University Press,.

Hume, D. 1978 [1740]. *A Treatise of Human Nature*. Oxford: Clarendon Press (originally published 1740).

Kane, R. 1996. *The Significance of Free Will*. Oxford: Oxford University Press.

Kant, I. 1996 [1787]. *Critique of Pure Reason*, W. Pluhar (trans.). Indianapolis, IN: Hackett (originally published 1787).

Kant, I. 1948. *Groundwork of the Metaphysics of Morals*, translated as *The Moral Law*, H. J. Paton (trans.) London: Hutchinson.

Kenny, A. 1968. *Descartes*. New York: Random House.

Kenny, A. 1992a. *The Metaphysics of Mind*. Oxford: Oxford University Press.

Kenny, A. 1992b. *What is Faith?* Oxford: Oxford University Press.

Locke, D. 1975. Three concepts of free action. *Proceedings of the Aristotelian Society*, supplementary volume, **XLIX**: 95–112.

Lucas, J. R. 1989. *The Future: An Essay on God, Temporality and Truth*. Oxford: Blackwell.

Lukes, S. 1973. *Individualism*. Oxford: Blackwell.

Mcfee, G. 1992. *Understanding Dance*. London: Routledge.

McGinn, C. 1999. *The Mysterious Flame: Conscious Minds in a Material World*. New York: Basic Books.

MacKay, D. 1967. *Freedom of Action in a Mechanistic Universe*. Cambridge: Cambridge University Press.

Mackie, J. L. 1974. *The Cement of the Universe*. Oxford: Clarendon.

Malthus, T. 1970 [1798] *An Essay on the Principle of Population*, A. Flew (ed.). Harmondsworth: Penguin (originally published 1798).

Melden, A. I. 1961. *Free Action*. London: Routledge & Kegan Paul.

Mellor, D. H. 1995. *The Facts of Causation*. London: Routledge.

Moore, G. E. 1959. *Philosophical Papers*. London: George Allen and Unwin.

Nagel, T. 1979. *Mortal Questions*. Cambridge: Cambridge University Press.

Nagel, T. 1986. *The View from Nowhere*. Oxford: Oxford University Press.

Nagel, T. 1995. *Other Minds: Critical Essays 1969–1994*. Oxford: Clarendon Press.

Nathan, N. M. L. 1992. *Will and World*. Oxford: Clarendon Press.

Nowell-Smith, P. H. 1954. *Ethics*. Harmondsworth: Penguin.

O'Connor, D. J. 1971. *Free Will*. London: Macmillan.

Passmore, J. 1961. *Philosophical Reasoning*. London: Duckworth.

Passmore, J. 1966. *One Hundred Years of Philosophy*. Harmondsworth: Penguin.

Pears, David (ed.) 1963. *Freedom and the Will*. London: Macmillan.

Pettit, P. 1993. A definition of physicalism. *Analysis* 55:141–6.

Popper, K. 1957. *The Poverty of Historicism*. London: Routledge.

Putnam, H. 1992. *Renewing Philosophy*. Cambridge, MA: Harvard University Press.

Quinton, A. 1973. *Utilitarian Ethics*. London: Macmillan.

Robinson, J. 1962. *Economic Philosophy*. London: Watts Press.

Ryle, G. 1949. *The Concept of Mind*. London: Hutchinson.

Salmon, W. 1974. Psychoanalytic theory and evidence. In *Philosophers on Freud: New Evaluations*, R. Wollheim (ed.), 271–84. New York: Jason Aaronson.

Sappington, A. A. 1990. Recent psychological approaches to the free will versus determinism issue. *Psychological Bulletin* 108: 1–11.

Schlick, M. 1966. When is a man responsible? In *Free Will and Determinism*, B. Berofsky (ed.), 54–63. New York: Harper & Row.

Scruton, R. 1982. *Kant*. Oxford: Oxford University Press.

Scruton, R. 1994. *Modern Philosophy: A Survey*. London: Sinclair-Stevenson.

Scruton, R. 1996. *An Intelligent Person's Guide To Philosophy*. London: Duckworth.

Searle, J. 1983. *Intentionality: An Essay in the Philosophy of Mind*. Cambridge: Cambridge University Press.

Shaw, P. 1981. *Logic and its Limits*. London: Pan Books.

Stebbing, S. 1937. *Philosophy and the Physicists*. Harmondsworth: Penguin.

Strawson, G. 1986. *Freedom and Belief*. Oxford: Clarendon.

Strawson, G. 1989. *The Secret Connection*. Oxford: Clarendon Press.

Strawson, P. 1959. *Individuals*. London: Methuen.

Strawson, P. 1974. *Freedom and Resentment, and Other Essays*. London: Methuen.

Stroud, B. 1984. *The Philosophical Significance of Scepticism*. Oxford: Clarendon Press.

Taylor, C. 1964. *The Explanation of Behaviour*. London: Routledge.

Thornton, M. 1989. *Do We Have Free Will?*. Bristol: Bristol Classical Press.

Toulmin, S. 1969. Concepts and the explanation of human behaviour. In *Human Action: Conceptual and Empirical Issues*, T. Mischel (ed.), 71–104. New York: Academic Press.

Travis, C. 1981. *The True and the False*. Amsterdam: John Benjamins.

Travis, C. 1989. *The Uses of Sense*. Oxford: Blackwell.

Travis, C. 1991. Annals of analysis. *Mind* 100: 237–64.

Trusted, J. 1984. *Free Will and Responsibility*. Oxford: Oxford University Press.

Van Inwagen, P. 1982. The incompatibility of free will and determinism. In *Free Will*, G. Watson (ed.), 46–58. Oxford: Oxford University Press.

Van Inwagen, P. 1983. *An Essay on Free Will*. Oxford: Clarendon Press.

Watson, G. (ed.) 1982. *Free Will*. Oxford: Oxford University Press.

White, A. (ed.) 1968. *The Philosophy of Action*. Oxford: Oxford University Press.

Wiggins, D. 1987. *Needs, Values, Truth*. Oxford: Blackwell.

Wilkerson, T. E. 1974. *Minds, Brains and People*. Oxford: Oxford University Press.

Williams, B. 1972. *Morality: An Introduction to Ethics*. Harmondsworth: Penguin.

Williams, B. 1985. *Ethics and the Limits of Philosophy*. London: Fontana.

Wisdom, J. 1953. *Philosophy and Psycho-analysis*. Oxford: Blackwell.

Wittgenstein, L. 1953. *Philosophical Investigations*. Oxford: Blackwell.

Wittgenstein, L. 1993. Lectures on freedom of the will. In his *Philosophical Occasions 1912–1951*, J. Klagge & A. Nordmann (eds), 427–44. Indianapolis, IN: Hackett.

Young, R. 1991. The implications of determinism. In *A Companion to Ethics*, P. Singer (ed.), 534–42. Oxford: Blackwell.

Index